Severn Gorge Countryside Trust manages most of the woodland and other countryside around Coalbrookdale, Ironbridge, Jackfield and Coalport, much of it within the World Heritage Site. The Trust works to conserve and enhance the landscape and its wildlife, whilst at the same time seeking to promote public access to the areas under its management. This is the real purpose of the present booklet, designed to interpret as widely as possible a very special area noted for its natural beauty, its nature conservation and remarkable industrial history.

The five largely circular routes described here offer a mix of walks. All of them contain a rich commentary on the associated history and social history, often with attendant stories and anecdotes. Three of the five are almost entirely on the level. One involves a very pleasant climb up to the traditionally-managed grassland of Haywood, whilst the Sutton Wood walk negotiates some steep sections. The walks are of varying length but can be joined up or shortened to suit the walker. What awaits you is an area of the Severn Gorge with a quite fascinating story to tell about its development, its landscape and ecology, and the human involvement in the story over a long period of time.

In many ways Jackfield and Coalport provide an interesting story of contrast, similarity and complement. Jackfield, to the south of the river Severn, was already an old established community before there was any thought of developing the area to the north and east of the river which became Coalport in the late 18C/early 19C. Indeed, Jackfield was one of the earliest riverside communities in this two-mile stretch of the Severn Gorge, long before Ironbridge came into existence. The village grew rather 'organically' and its somewhat sprawling and disjointed nature is still in evidence today. Most of this is due not so much to the usual ebb and flow of an industrial riverside development, as the profound physical disruption caused by the coming of the railway in the mid-19C, the calamity of a major landslip in the 20C, and to programmes of 'slum clearance' which removed historic parts of the settlement. The basis of Jackfield's industrial development was the generous mineral resources of coal and clay which which were exploited throughout its history. This is particularly true of its pottery industry, which grew up from very early times and may well have exported skills and experience to the Potteries in nearby Staffordshire. If the area produced on the whole rather prosaic, domestic ware, it did, in time, develop a much sought-after distinctive black-glazed earthenware. It also acquired considerable demand for its brick and roof tile products, although a far greater reputation is based upon the decorative tile industry which became established in late-Victorian times and continued throughout the first half of the 20C. Some of the most beautiful tiles in the world were made in this little village.

Coalport, by way of contrast, was very much a planned 'new town', the inspiration of the ironmaster and entrepreneur William Reynolds. At its height it was a busy and prosperous place, although its growth was always limited and never came to fulfil the aspirations of its founder or his executors. There were plans to develop the wharfage much more extensively, and to build an ambitious chemical industry which never got off the ground at all. It did, however, establish a wonderful clay china industry, and Coalport china very quickly acquired a national and international reputation. Such standing derived not only from the quality of its porcelain but also that of its design and decoration.

Like many of the industrialists of the area, William Reynolds and his successors knew how essential it was to provide housing for his workforce, and some of the rows of workers' cottages from that time remain in Coalport. However, the Coalport china industry proved for the greater part of its history so successful that most of its workforce was consistently drawn from the much bigger communities of Jackfield and Broseley to the south, getting to and from Coalport each day via the ferry.

Today, the landscape context for the two communities is one of woodland on the valley slopes. At the eastern end of Jackfield are Preenshead and Corbett's Dingle, ancient woodland in origin but which appears to have been clear-felled in the late 1940s. Behind Coalport is Haywood, formerly meadow and pasture land of Hay Farm, owned in the 18C by the Quaker industrialists, the Darby Family, and which today is composed of meadow and woodland, mostly of larch, giving a fine continuous display of gold in autumn. Sutton Wood, further east, appears to be largely replanted ancient woodland, nowadays with stands of relatively young conifers and mixed broadleaf species. Both of these stretches of woodland form a continuity with that further west, such as at Benthall Edge at the southern end of Ironbridge itself. Unlike that fine woodland, however, little of Preenshead, Haywood and Sutton Wood appears to have been greatly affected by industrial development in the past. These are all now managed by the Severn Gorge Countryside Trust.

Early records of the Jackfield area date from medieval times when fish weirs were constructed at naturally shallow points in the river Severn. Ferry crossings were also important. One of the earliest crossing was known as Adams Ferry, on the site of the present day Free Bridge.

Nowadays, Jackfield is usually noted as one of the communities that comprise the Ironbridge Gorge, but for the greater part of its history it was a distinct industrial village in its own right, thriving long before Ironbridge was even thought of. Indeed, the village grew up as a string of little clusters, each with its own name, characteristics and reasons for coming into being. 'Jack-Field', for example, was simply a district noted for its pottery manufacture. The accessibility of local mineral resources from early times and the transport opportunities of the river Severn prompted the creation of wharves. The various riverside settlements soon became established: Ladywood, Coalford, Lloyds Head, Calcutts, Ash Tree, Salthouses, The Tuckies, The Werps are all distinct parts of Jackfield. If the number of these different neighbourhoods is anything to go by, there can be few villages as

complex and as indicative of the rich and varied commerce that distinguished the place from early times. In the 18C Jackfield is said to have shown many of the characteristics of a small hustling seaport with its inns and alehouses, its brothels, and terraces of workers' cottages. It was a crowded place, full of life. Many of the lodging houses were for itinerant bargemen and bow-haulers, whose work was wretched and brutalising, and who were considered particularly disreputable. By the late-18C the village had a rather hardened outlook on life and something of a seedy reputation. Nowadays, it is a quiet, somewhat disjointed settlement reflecting the many changes of its industrial past, not to mention the physical consequences of a major landslip in modern times.

Early-18C map of 'Jack-Field' showing pottery works and rail system down to the river side

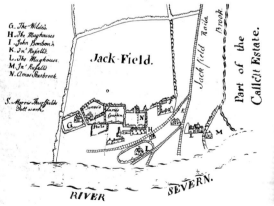

There are still a handful of fine houses from its former prosperity, but of the twenty three public houses which the village once boasted, only *The Black Swan, The Boat* and *The Station Hotel* survive.

Black Jackfield mug

alehouse itself. Jackfield pottery came to acquire its own distinctive forms, particularly its slipware and black-glazed ware, now highly sought-after and known simply as Jackfield ware.

An early-18C hand-drawn estate map of the Calcutts at 'Jack-Field' reveals that by this time the district's pottery industry was already well established. At least three Jackfield potteries are identified, two referred to as mughouses ('muggusses' in the local dialect), probably making simple earthenware items for domestic use. The term 'mug' may have been a drinking vessel used in the alehouses, so that the term 'mughouse' also became a local synonym for the

The Calcutts riverside shown on the map is also notable as the site of a large and impressive ironworks in the late-18C, operated by one Alexander Brodie. Surviving archaeology for ironworks on this side of the river is not extensive, but there was good quality ore to be had and it is known that historically there were many such works. Brodie's factory, however, was a quite exceptional enterprise. It produced huge quantities of cannon, deployed during the Napoleonic Wars,

Early brickmaking enterprise

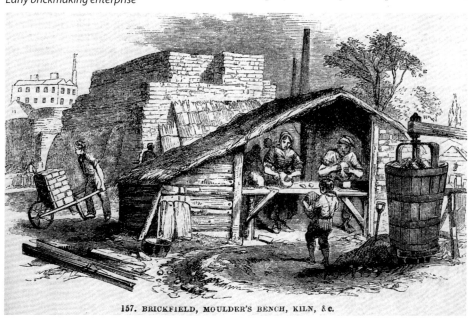

157. BRICKFIELD, MOULDER'S BENCH, KILN, &c.

two such pieces of ordnance being commissioned for Nelson's HMS Victory. The steam-driven boring mills could bore 10 cannon at once, a spectacle which the Prince & Princess of Orange were treated to on a Royal visit to the Gorge in 1796

Jackfield, however, is best noted for its clay industries of brickmaking, roof tilemaking and decorative tiles. The development of these industries provided a huge market for local coal, whilst in turn the ready availability of the mineral fuelled the prosperity of the clay industry. The earliest brickmaking concern appears to have begun in the Coalford area in the late-17C but it was probably the better part of another century before brickmaking moved from the simple, casual hand-made operations on site, to the industrialised processes of the brickworks using relatively sophisticated equipment and employing a great many people. At a time when much of the Gorge was characterised by industrial decline, brickworks continued to increase. The key to this surprising growth lay in the development of the clay roof tile industry, such tiles often being fired in the kilns simultaneously with bricks. 'Roof tile' bricks show characteristic dark diagonal banding where the ends of stacked tiles have been fired, leaving their imprint. Examination of almost any 18C/19C house in the Ironbridge Gorge shows examples of such bricks. The roofs, too, are almost universally tiled with local products.

Throughout the 19C Jackfield clay roofing tiles acquired a national reputation, huge quantities sent for export via the river, and, after the 1860s, by rail. The tiles in question were extremely hardwearing with a dark, purple-brown or brindled appearance made from local Broseley clay. This was regarded by the manufacturers as unique and the product was jealously guarded against imitation. The industry declined in the late-19C for a number of reasons. Fashions changed in the type and colour of tile demanded and the use of other local clays failed to reproduce the quality required. The opening up of the railways meant that there was also the incursion of new materials into the market such as slate. Not least of the problems, however, was the introduction of machine-made tiles which affected quality badly. The industry survived into the 20C but labour shortages associated with two World Wars eventually closed the chapter for good. Today, there are few reminders of the industry with the exception of

Remarkable retaining wall in Jackfield partly composed of old saggars, used to protect the delicate china during kiln firing

the ubiquitous tile waste tips all over Jackfield, holding up sections of river embankments, and numerous other retaining walls, including garden walls.

The clay industry, however, which perhaps best reveals the skill and industry and reputation of Jackfield is its manufacture of decorative tiles.

Those tiles having an impressed pattern infilled with clay of a different colour are known as encaustic tiles, and were first introduced into Britain in the 13C. There is evidence to suggest local clays were used in precisely this type of early medieval floor tile in nearby Buildwas Abbey. However, it wasn't until the great Victorian designers, restorers and architects, such as Augustus Pugin, began to demand decorative encaustic tiles that the industry took off and Jackfield became home to two of the finest manufactories.

By 1874 the new purpose-built tile manufactory of Craven Dunhill & Co. had been laid out in the village on the site of an early pottery, and the company began producing mock medieval designs and art pottery, the latter in response to the Arts & Crafts movement of the period. In fact, this movement was critical of mass production, but Craven Dunhill as well as its much larger rivals Maw & Co were hugely successful - as was the Victorian decorative tile industry as a whole – because they supplied what the market required and made products that were

as fine as those of the artist-craftsman. Craven Dunhill continued production until the mid-20C and today the handsome Victorian building is home to the Jackfield Tile Museum, where specialist tiles are still made.

In 1852 George and Arthur Maw had started an encaustic tile manufactory in nearby Benthall, taking advantage of the qualities of local clays which they were familiar with from their former Worcester factory. The Benthall site soon became cramped and in 1883 they moved to Jackfield to set up another new purpose-built factory, also designed to use steam-driven  machinery. Maw & Co was some three times the size of the Craven Dunhill factory and in its day became the largest encaustic tile manufactory in the world. It employed hundreds of workers, produced millions of tiles each year, and played a huge part in the economic and, to some extent, the social prosperity of the area. Both of these two major tile companies produced tiles that came to adorn such public buildings as town halls, churches, libraries, railway stations, schools, public houses, and many private houses both at home and in far-flung corners of the world. Like Craven Dunhill, Maw & Co suffered from the depression which set in after the Second World War, but did continue on until 1969.

One of the reasons that both Craven Dunhill and Maw & Co decided on brand new architect-designed sites for their tile enterprises involved the fact that the Severn Valley Railway had recently been constructed, opening in 1862. Both companies had dedicated sidings and were sited to take advantage of all of the transport opportunities offered by the railway.

Although Jackfield never had its own proper station, it did have a 'Halt' (moved further down line, following the landslip of 1952) and the railway became as important to the life of the community as anywhere else. Its construction also had a profoundly disruptive effect on the village, many houses being swept away with its arrival. The promise of building replacement dwellings was never honoured.

However, not even the physical impact on the village caused by the railway could compare to the calamity which overtook the community in 1952 when a spectacular landslip occurred in the Salthouses district which virtually created two communities. The news made the national dailies for a fortnight. There were further slips, most notably in April 1983 when the Salthouse Road slid into the river, and a section of the former bed of the

railway became the adopted road. Even that is unstable to the point where the County Council has had to resort to the use of pinned wooden planks which are repaired or renewed at regular intervals and which has become known as Jackfield's famous 'tank track' or 'wooden road.'

In so far as Coalport's fame is based upon its use of clay, there is an obvious connection with the experiences of Jackfield, although the sources of material and the uses to which they were put were distinct. Jackfield's industrial wealth was derived from its own local clays, whereas that used at Coalport to make china was largely imported from Cornwall. In a sense the relationship was always close between the two neighbouring communities, albeit ones divided by the river. Jackfield was much the bigger community, supplied workers to Coalport's famous china works, and

Engraving of early 19C Coalport China Works

also offered perhaps greater social and shopping opportunities

Coalport was very much the inspiration of the ironmaster William Reynolds and the key to its development lay in the canal/river interchange which he instigated in the late-18C.

In 1788 the ironmaster began work on the all-important canal/river interchange on land abutting the river, a place described as *'poor meadow... which could scarcely support even grass'*. However, it was land, once developed, that was to prove critical to the emergence of Coalport. The East Shropshire canal was in the process of being built to the north and the challenge was how to connect this upper section of canal when it arrived at Blists Hill to the river, some 207 feet (63m) below. A competition was held and in 1792 the adoption of an astonishing engineering construction called the Hay Inclined Plane, still considered one of Britain's foremost industrial monuments. For more than a hundred years it moved goods and raw materials between the upper section of the East Shropshire canal at Blist's Hill and the River Severn below.

Once the canal system in its entirety had been linked to the river, goods and raw material began to move. William Reynolds set about promoting this new basin at the canal/river interchange, encouraging new industries to locate there. Soon wharves, workshops, and terraces of workers' cottages were built.

William Reynolds, founder of Coalport

Reynolds also built a huge stone warehouse, spanning the canal onto the river. This has long since been demolished there are surviving sandstone blocks on the river embankment where it formerly stood. By 1794 the area was being referred to as 'Coalport' and the planned 'new town' had begun to grow up.

By far the most famous and enduring enterprise at Coalport was its china industry. Over the course of time, there were a number of different works, producing different wares. Most notable of these, however, was the china works established by John Rose.

Rose first set up business with a partner in Jackfield in 1793 making china there for three years before crossing the river to set up a new china works. Like others, he presumably had recognised the potential of the new development being promoted by William Reynolds.

By 1796 the factory was in operation, employing a workforce of a hundred people under one roof, an indication of how the revolutionary changes in the Severn valley had already transformed the scale of industry from the domestic context to the large factory. Within the next few years, Rose and his partners prospered to such an extent that in the first years of the 19C his firm was described as 'the largest and most expensive porcelain producing estate in Great Britain'. The rapid growth of the company, however, appears to have been unhealthy. In 1803 Rose and his partner, Blakeway, were bankrupt, although Rose himself was subsequently appointed manager of the china works by the new owners. The company prospered sufficiently to buy out its competitors, Anstice, Horton & Rose (Thomas Rose, brother to John) who had built a china works on the south side of the canal. In 1814 the two companies were merged and ultimately became known as John Rose & Co. It continued as such for the remainder of the 19C, though not without periods of changing fortunes.

Rose was responsible for many changes, expanding the business considerably and taking out many new patents.

The Great War of 1914 spelt a huge blow to the china trade. Coalport, which was a relatively isolated community away from the main centres of population was particularly vulnerable and suffered declining markets. In the 18C proximity to the river Severn had always provided a vital transport link, and a comparative industrial advantage.

By the 19C, however, the wholesale development of the canal system and the early arrival of the railways elsewhere, began to make the manufacturing areas vulnerable to competition. The Gorge in general, and Coalport in particular, had already begun to become more isolated. Cutbacks, wage reductions, and industrial unrest led eventually to closure. In 1926 the company was sold off and production transferred to the Potteries where china still bearing the Coalport 'imprint' is made as part of the Wedgwood Group. In 1967 the derelict factory site became the highly successful 'Coalport China Museum'.

The arrival in the Gorge by the 1860s of two standard guage railways was seen as the way of arresting decline. By 1862

The close of Coalport China Works in 1926

Coalport could boast two such railway lines with stations on opposite sides of the river, no mean achievement for such a relatively tiny community! In 1860 the London & North Western Railway (L&NWR) arrived with its station on the north side of the river, while two years later the Great Western Railway (GWR) Severn Valley Railway ran on the south side.

Certainly, the China Works took advantage of this new method of transport, and the new passenger trains also offered social, recreational and shopping opportunities for local people, especially to the market towns of Wellington and Oakengates. Within a few years, however, the effect on river traffic (which had been in decline, anyway) was considerable, and the sole survivor of the Severn trows - 'The William' - sailed down to Bristol with its cargo of roof tiles for the last time in 1885. As elsewhere in the Gorge, Coalport enjoyed the advantages of its railway services for just about a hundred years. Today, the

The Coalport 'Dodger' preparing to leave Coalport East Station circa 1950. Notice the cattle truck, there being a cattle 'dock' at Coalport for the local farms.

Opening of the Memorial Bridge in 1922 by Lord & Lady Forester

beds of the old railway lines have been converted into major recreational routes at a local and national level for walkers and cyclists.

In 1922 perhaps the most unusual and useful memorial to the dead of the First World War, subsequently rededicated to the fallen of both World Wars, was proposed and financed by public subscription. The Coalport & Jackfield Memorial Bridge for pedestrians finally came to replace the Coalport (or Werps or Jackfield) ferry which had dutifully plied between the two communities ever since the need had arisen with the arrival of Coalport. At once the bridge provided the many workers from Jackfield with an easier and safer means of getting to and from work.

In the end Coalport exhausted its chapter as a distinct manufacturing centre. It was successful because it linked to the river Severn the other industries of the Gorge, and in particular the land-locked towns and industry of the northern parts of the East Shropshire Coalfield. By the time the railways came to replace the often difficult and unreliable use of the Severn, the Gorge as a whole was already in industrial decline and the railways could not be expected to reverse such a process, especially when the major centres of industry were being established elsewhere. Today, the village is a quiet rural backwater whose pleasant riverside setting and rich industrial heritage draw many visitors to it. They come to take in the atmosphere, perhaps to feel something of its former life – to imagine for themselves how differently the place must have once appeared, and smelt and sounded by dint of its many industries.

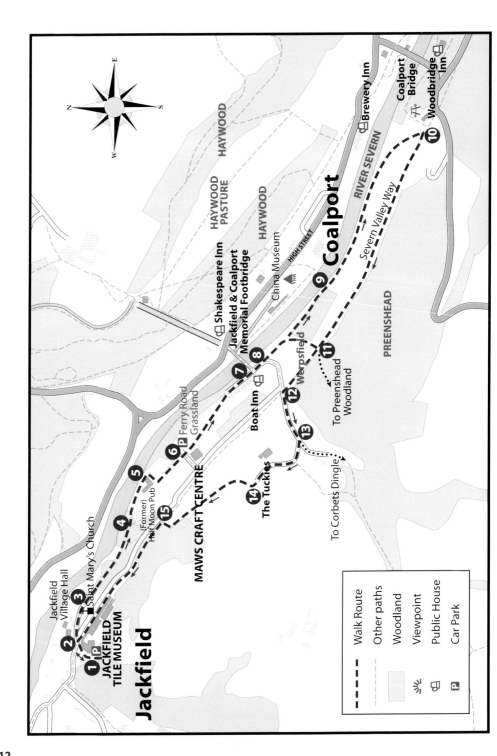

Jackfield

Coalport

RIVER SEVERN

HAYWOOD

HAYWOOD PASTURE

HAYWOOD

PREENSHEAD

Brewery Inn

Coalport Bridge

Woodbridge Inn

Severn Valley Way

Shakespeare Inn

Jackfield & Coalport Memorial Footbridge

China Museum

HIGH STREET

YHA

Boat Inn

Werpsfield

To Preenshead Woodland

Ferry Road Grassland

To Corbets Dingle

The Tuckies

(Former) Half Moon Pub

MAWS CRAFT CENTRE

Saint Mary's Church

Jackfield Village Hall

JACKFIELD TILE MUSEUM

Jackfield

— — — Walk Route

– – – Other paths

Woodland

Viewpoint

Public House

Car Park

Jackfield Tile Museum to Salthouses to The Werps to Severn Valley Way to The Tuckies

Starting from Jackfield Tile Museum (car park nearby), this walk takes in a good slice of Jackfield's remarkable history, including **an early lodging house, a distinctive church, former tile works, and a 19C pub next to the old ferry crossing.** From here the walk continues along the riverside, offering fine views of **Coalport and its bridge,** before returning along the line of the former **Severn Valley Railway.** The walk concludes by exploring a fascinating stretch of the old **Tuckies** community with the oldest house of any size within the Gorge.

🚶 **Accessibility:** Boots are essential all year round for frequent muddy sections on this walk, particularly in winter. The walk is mostly on the level and involves negotiating a number of stiles and/or gates. Two sections run alongside the river - children will need to be supervised.

🌾 **Key Features:** Industrial, social and cultural history, archaeology, viewpoints.

🕐 **Length & Time:** About 3.5km, about 2 hours (2.5km, 1¼ hours for shorter option)

🚌 **Public Transport:** Buses to Jackfield (Calcutts Road) and nearby Ironbridge & Coalport

🍴 **Refreshments:** Black Swan and Boat Inn, cafés at Jackfield Tile Musuem and Maw's Craft Centre

🚻 **Toilets:** At pubs in Jackfield, Jackfield Tile Museum, Maw's Craft Centre, also in Ironbridge.

1 With the front of the Tile Museum on your right, cross directly over the road into Church Road.

Opposite the Tile Museum is the former Church of England Jackfield School, bearing the date 1843. The Tile Museum itself occupies a handsome high-Victorian building which was formerly Craven Dunhill Encaustic Tile Works, one of two large decorative tile manufacturers within half a mile of each other. The other was Maw & Co further down the valley. Both of these enterprises quickly acquired national and international reputations from the late 19C, and their success meant that some of the world's most beautiful tiles were made in this little village of Jackfield.

2 As you take a few steps down Church Road towards the church, cast your eyes to the left, below road level, to a white-rendered house named the 'Severn Trow'.

Parts of this private dwelling are very old indeed, and its remarkable history can be read about on Page 16.
Continue walking down Church Road towards St. Mary's Church.

MEMORIES OF GROWING UP IN JACKFIELD IN THE 1940s

"I went to Jackfield School, like everyone round here. During the Second World War, I remember Craven Dunhill's was given over to the War Effort and in class you'd often hear a great deal of clanking of metal parts coming from the factory, and even Sten guns being fired on land behind the school to test them. Of course, we never knew what was going on during the war because you weren't allowed to ask or find out. There were no photos because we weren't allowed to take them. But we knew that most of the brick and tile factories - closed for the duration of the war and never re-opened - were being used as ammunition stores, though precisely where and what was being stored we didn't know. A lot of the time we were frightened because German planes were constantly overhead. There was a huge petrol store at Farley, not far away. They used to run a late train here about

10.30pm, so that its steam wasn't visible. We would listen to it going by in the night. I can't recall much about the brick and tile works. They were just a feature of the area. There were two lovely horses that worked at Doughty's Brick & Tile Works, bringing down the tiles to the railway in little wheeled carts or trucks. The man further down the village loved those horses and treated them wonderfully.

When I was a young girl of about eight or so, I used to get on the GWR train at The Halt above **The Boat Inn** and travel down to Coalport Station, get off and go to the Bridge Inn, now the Woodbridge Hotel. My auntie and some other relatives used to run it in those days. People would quite often take the GWR train to Coalport station, cross the bridge if they wanted to go to Coalport. CONTINUED OVERLEAF

There were many shops in the village. There was a little wooden shop until a few years ago, run by Norman Poole, near where they've preserved a bit of the old Free Bridge. There was a shop in 'The Square' next to the Bull Ring, just down from **The Black Swan**. There was another in Church Road, just this side of the church. It's still there, covered in ivy. We've decided that's the only way to protect what we've got, keep them covered in ivy! Down the road, near the Half Moon pub, there was another, proper 'Square' with a shop and the Post Office. When that was demolished after the landslip of the 1950s, another shop opened up near the church. We used to have quite a few shops, including a fish and chip shop.

When the landslip came and people were being moved out to Broseley, many is the time I've cried as a young woman, thinking I would be sent to live in Broseley. There was a real sense of community in Jackfield in those days, and the village was so much more a village. I must say I resent the fact that

those who don't know much about the place or anything of its history are often belittling of things we struggled and fought to get, like the Village Hall, for example, next to the Severn Trow. What it cost us to get that built! Actually, it was the same with most things here. The church was built out of public donation, same with the Coalport & Jackfield Memorial footbridge. In those days a great many things went on in the life of the village. There was the JADS, for example, the Jackfield Amateur Dramatic Society. They used to put on lots of plays and pantomimes, all in the area. Now, nothing."

The church of St. Mary the Virgin even at a casual glance can be seen to be a highly original building. It was consecrated in 1863, built to a design by Arthur Blomfield who was then a student of the far greater architect, William Butterfield, designer of Keble College, Oxford. The influence of that building on the design of St. Mary's is evident. As with so many of Jackfield's expressions of pride in its community, and a testament to its fundraising abilities, the church was built entirely by public donation. It uses local materials extensively, many of which were provided by John Doughty, a church dignitary and notable brick and tile manufacturer. Brick types of several colours are deployed in unusual patterning. There are columns of local terracotta by the door, and supporting the spire. It also has the oddity of two semi-circular apses at the east end. A further curiosity - whether by accident or 'design' - involves one of the stained glass panels depicting the

Crucifixion, being set in reverse which gives a rather strange appearance of "floating heads" and headless bodies. The churchyard itself at the western end has a lovely multi-stemmed box tree, unusual to find for a plant which is almost always used for hedging. Opposite the church is Jackfield Village Hall, built once again by public subscription, on the site of the bowling green of the former *Severn Trow* public house.

St Mary's Church, Jackfield

3 Continue down Church Road. The metalled road ends rather abruptly after a few more metres with some bollards. However, it is possible to continue down a track, slightly off to the left. As you walk along, the path at one point approaches the riverbank from where a sense of some of Jackfield's famous 'rapids' can be appreciated. You may also notice on the path, small sections of tarmac, or concrete, or brickwork, especially off to the right, and a general awareness of severely disturbed ground.

The reason that the path is so disturbed is that you are actually walking along the remains of the old Salthouse Road, the main road into the once-vibrant district of Jackfield known as Salthouses. Most of the district was lost as a consequence of a calamitous landslips in 1952.

THE SEVERN TROW: Story of a Remarkable Lodging House, Brothel, Public House, Village Hall, Public Library

The Severn Trow came to play a fascinating part in the industrial and social history of Jackfield. Built probably back in the 16C, some experts have even suggested it may have been one of the very earliest brick-built houses in Shropshire (one brick bears the date 1601). Almost certainly the present-day building reflects construction at different times throughout the centuries.

A very early part may have had a simple bottle kiln and draught chamber, one of a number of early pottery 'mughouses' known to be in Jackfield. The main house, however, appears to have been built or served as a

CONTINUED OVERLEAF

lodging house for itinerant barge workers when Jackfield had much of the character of a bustling seaport. Some of the larger barges had sails and were known as trows. These were both graceful and robust working vessels which plied their trade up and down the river, Bristol being a major port in the winter months when the river was navigable that far.

Most of the men who used lodging houses such as the Severn Trow were bow haulers, gangs of 6 or 8 men who pulled the barges upstream. Each day they walked the riverbank (rugged and unmade) from one lodging house to the next, a distance known as a 'length'. It was hard, brutalising work and bow haulers were regarded as particularly disreputable. Contemporary observers, however, agreed that the work itself was degrading. The 18C Methodist minister John Fletcher was particularly moved by the wretchedness of these men:

"How they are bathed in sweat and rain. Fastened to their lines as horses to their traces, wherein do they differ from the laborious brutes? Not in erect posture of the body, for in the intenseness of their toil, they bend forward, their head foremost, and their hand upon the ground. If there is any difference it consists in this: horses are indulged with a collar to save their breasts; and these; as if theirs were not worth saving draw without one; the beasts tug in patient silence and mutual harmony; but the men with loud contention and horrible imprecations. "

In the late 18C a proper towpath was constructed along the river, bow hauling by men was outlawed and the work subsequently undertaken with more dignity by horses.

In reality from its beginnings the Severn Trow - as with other such buildings - was rather more than just a lodging house: it also operated as a brothel and a licensed alehouse with brewing occurring on the premises. Here, it seems, most of the needs of its clients were catered for under one roof. Moreover, barge workers were often effectively 'tied' to their masters, since they were paid in tokens which they were obliged to spend at the establishments owned by their masters.

The Severn Trow probably pre-dated any significant roads into Jackfield and entrance to the house was therefore directly from the riverfront with its wharfs and moored barges. Today, the front of the house (off Church Road) is its former back, and although it has been restored and modernised, much of the original layout has survived. Downstairs is the original vaulted brewhouse (possibly an adaptation of the bottle kiln's draught chamber), the parlour and the bar; upstairs is the 44' long former dormitory with its rows of bunk beds. Opposite is another room with what appears to have had partitioning for a series of brothel cubicles!

Within a decade or two of the coming of the railway to the Ironbridge Gorge in 1862 the river traffic was swept away. The traditional uses of lodging houses such as the Severn Trow changed. It continued to operate as an inn, with its full liquor license until the early years of the 20C when scandal overtook its publican. Henry Potts, a married man with children, was a prominent member of the church of St. Mary's just down the road from the Severn Trow. His compromising of a 16-year-old local girl scandalised the

Jackfield community and he was hounded out of the village. The Church then bought the house with some suggestion that Henry Potts himself, or his father who may have been the mortgagee, offered it to the Church, provided it took on the relatively small outstanding mortgage. For awhile the Church continued to run the Severn Trow as a licensed inn, a fact which caused some considerable disquiet in Church circles. The licence was eventually worked out and the building consecrated for church services and meetings, thereby inaugurating a new chapter in the life of a building which contrasted starkly with its former uses!

Even before the Church took over the Severn Trow, part of the building was already functioning as a public library for the people of Jackfield. It is conceivable that this had begun in the 19C as one of 'Mudie's Select Library' outlets, a hugely successful subscription library which grew to become prominent nationally before its demise in the late 19C. More likely, however, to account for the large number of Mudie's books in the Jackfield library, is the suggestion that these were bought up when Mudie's closed. Presumably, the Church continued to administer the library after the pub's delicensing and it appears to have been still functioning as late as the early 1960s.

The Severn Trow served other social and welfare functions for the community under the Church's direction.

Over the succeeding years it became the meeting place for the local Sea Scouts troupe, the Mother's Union, the Sunday School, and, later, in the huge former dormitory room, it comprised an ad hoc Village Hall, before the Village Hall proper of St. Mary's was built on the site of the Severn Trow's former bowling green. During this period in the early 20C in one of the bedrooms of the house there was also a resource known as 'Jackfield Comfort's Cupboard'. This was a community resource - paid for by small donations from the residents of the village - which provided the loan of such basic items as bedpans, rubber sheets, hot water bottles, even a steam kettle for respiratory complaints - perhaps due to the high dust levels in the brickworks and tile works, or perhaps complaints associated with living so close to the river, sometimes referred to as 'Jackfield Lung'!

The Severn Trow can be seen then to have played a huge part in the life of Jackfield throughout its history. In relatively recent years the house fell into dilapidation, narrowly escaped a demolition order, before being sold into private ownership and its subsequent restoration.

4 You will soon exit from the scrub woodland into a large cleared area. Ahead of you is a half-timbered building, the former Half Moon pub, with a road off to the right. This road was built as a service road - used publicly nonetheless - to the major tile manufacturer, Maw & Co. It was noted for its straightness and acquired the local name of 'The Mekest' *(see page 20)* with an interesting derivation. However, we shall continue instead on the track round to the left, in front of the former Half Moon pub.

The Jackfield Slip: Village On The Move

In early April 1952 Jackfield hit the national daily newspapers for a fortnight. The reason? A spectacular landslip in the Salthouses district of the village. The affected area was a significant district in Jackfield with its Half Moon pub, the post office, a shop and numerous houses forming part of 'The Square'. Some of the earliest indications of how serious the problem had become was sounded when the General Post Office stopped its postmen using the main road into the district. Houses began cracking apart, and started to lean at drunken angles. Trees and lamp-posts were uprooted, garden walls keeled over, and the railway line was so badly undermined that after the passage of each train its 'near tottering' state had to be shored up by gangs of men with ballast before the next could gingerly negotiate the line. The lower section of Salthouse Road in the area between St. Mary's Church and the pub, became an impassable switchback with 10 feet [3m] humps. The landslip effectively split the village in two, and all but a tiny part of an old and vital part of the village was demolished, its residents rehoused outside of the district.

The land in the Salthouse area in particular

had always been on the move but the process had been gradual. Something had tipped the balance and the consensus was that the culprit lay with old mine workings on the hillsides. Once the mines had closed, following the Second World War, and water was no longer being pumped out, water levels built up to such an extent that the upper clay measures simply gave way against the harder bed clays.

The slippage continued and the experts gave their gloomy prognostications. Alderman Tom Wedge told the local council at the time: 'We must resign ourselves to the fact that the whole of the village will one day disappear.'

Jackfield appears to have survived to date. However, some twenty years after the first major slip, on the 30th April 1983 the ground was on the move again and this time more of the Salthouse Road slipped into the river along with the sewer, gas and water

CONTINUED OVERLEAF

mains. The bed of the former railway track (closed in 1963) then became the adopted road but this had already shown itself prone to distorting earlier and did so again. The County Council in desperation laid a series of wooden boards, pegged with steel straps, along the worst section of the road, keeping the main services alongside the road above ground for maintenance purposes. Today Jackfield's famous wooden road just about holds together but requires constant maintenance. The area around it bears no relation to how it once was, as with so many other parts of the village.

THE "MEKEST"

The road structure through the district of Jackfield known as the Salthouses has undergone many changes over the centuries, not least those due to the spectacular landslips of April 1952. One of the roads which junctioned with Church Road was built by Maw's Works as a service road, though it was used publicly, and was known as Maw's Private Top Road. It ran in a straight line to the Maw's Tile Works, so straight that the Maw's Work's factory chimney could be seen from the edge of St. Mary's churchyard. Children learnt to ride their bicycles along it, and mothers could keep an eye on their children playing. It was used by Jackfield School for its races and relays because the straightness of the road foiled any attempts at cheating! The road was also known as the "Mekest", meaning the "Make-Haste". When the morning siren sounded at Craven Dunhill's Tile Works, you knew there were only about five minutes before Maw's would sound theirs. And if you weren't there on time, the gates were locked, and you'd forfeited a day's wages.

The Half Moon pub was one of two notable riverside drinking establishments in Jackfield (the other being *The Boat Inn*, still thriving, further downstream) with a good deal of healthy rivalry between them, and both seriously prone to flooding. The Half Moon closed in 1997.

5 Continue past the former pub for a few metres and take the first narrow path off to the right and subsequently left into a narrow lane which is Salthouse Road.

On your left is a row of cottages, known as Severn Terrace. These are Victorian replacements of much earlier dwellings. In one surviving cellar there is reputed to still exist an example of the salt pans which were supplied from early times by natural salt springs in the area. The district of Salthouses grew up as a consequence of its early pottery industry, possibly using its salt to make salt-glazed earthenware, a technique known at least from Anglo-Saxon times.

6 The narrow lane you have just walked up soon exits into the open. There is a car park off to the left, and to the right the surviving buildings of Maw & Co's huge decorative tile works. These have been converted into an enterprising Craft Centre and are well worth a visit either now or at the end of your walk.

THE HALF MOON JUG

Up until the late 1980s, outside the door of the former Half Moon Inn stood a gigantic earthenware jug. The story goes that during the 1890s an unlikely challenge took place between the landlord and some of his customers, most of whom were from Maw's Works and who were often after a free pint or two. Thinking to satisfy their importuning once and for all, and at no great cost to himself, the landlord said if they brought their own jug, he would fill it up for free. So, they got together at the Works and made the biggest jug they could manage. They transported it down the back of Severn Terrace on a hand cart.

An alternative version of the story has it that the jug is very old indeed, made at the Ash Tree Pottery which was demolished to make way for the Victorian Craven Dunhill Tile Works in 1874. Once again, the landlord is said to have agreed he would fill with beer any jug that the workers could make that would hold a barrel's worth.

It must have held easily eight or nine gallons. Though a considerable shock to the landlord, he honoured his word. In turn, the workers presented the jug to him as a gift. It stood outside the pub as a feature on display for years. Then, one day in the floods which followed the big freeze of 1946, the jug was carried away by the river and subsequently broken. Some enterprising people found quite a lot of the sherds and reassembled them, filling in the missing parts with concrete, strapped up the restored jug with old barrel hoops and mounted it on a brick plinth.

Following the closure of the pub in 1984, suggestions were put forward for relocating the jug in a museum. When the pub briefly reopened the new owners donated the jug to the Ironbridge Gorge Museum Trust. They, in turn, commissioned Ms. Lesley Durbin to restore and reconstruct it to its former glory. It is now on permanent display at the Jackfield Tile Museum.

George and Arthur Maw began manufacturing Patent Encaustic Tiles in Worcester in 1850, importing clay from the Benthall area of the Ironbridge Gorge. The logic of actually moving close to the source of the clay, and also to an area with an already established clay industry, persuaded them to look for suitable premises which they found at Benthall in 1852 on the site of a former ironworks. The success and expansion of the business soon led to another move to the nearby Tuckies district of Jackfield where, in 1883, they opened a purpose-built factory, designed by Charles Lynham (who also designed the Craven Dunhill works). Maw's new factory took advantage of the latest techniques in tile manufacture and also crucially the proximity of the Severn Valley Railway, recently constructed in 1862. Today, although extensive, the surviving buildings convey nothing of the sheer scale of the company at its height. The works literally dwarfed the surroundings and became the largest and most modern tile factory in the world. It employed over 400 workers, produced some 20 million tiles per annum, and counted amongst its illustrious clients Tsar Alexander II of Russia, the Queen of Egypt, the Maharaja of Mysore and numerous others. Its products were eagerly promoted by such architects as the gothic revivalist, Augustin Pugin. Maw's tiles, as with those of Craven Dunhill, found their way not only into churches but into

libraries, railway stations, local and national government buildings, and increasingly private dwellings. The years following the Second World War ushered in an entirely different economic climate, one of depression coupled with changing fashions which began to signal the company's decline. It struggled on for a number of years but eventually closed for business in Jackfield in 1969. Maw's tiles are still made under that name in the Potteries.

Continue on to the path at the side of Maw's Craft Centre, with the car park on your left, and a pleasant landscaped green area. As you walk down, the great brick factory wall of Maw's is on your right.

The amenity grassland to your left conveys nothing of its history. In fact, much of it is comprised of huge quantities of ceramic tile waste. Particularly after the devastating floods of 1795, the building up of the river bank was much encouraged and Maw's dumped thousands of tonnes of such waste over the years. Much to the dismay of local parents, it is recalled that in the early decades of the 20C children were regularly attracted to the river's edge to crunch over the tiles and use them for skimming practice. Towards the end of this path, you will notice a preserved wooden chute emerging from the Maw's factory wall on the right. It was designed to be at such a height that a horse and cart could fit conveniently beneath it. The mechanism was self-acting, so that when tile waste was tipped into the chute from the factory above, the trap door opened to fill the cart, and sprang back into place afterwards.

The 'green' also had a number of buildings on it in the past. An aerial photo of Jackfield taken in the summer of 1948 reveals that there were cottages on the land, and the Maw's canteen, known as the "Mess Room" which also once served as the Village Hall. There was even a tennis court, reflecting something of the commitment of the company to the social welfare of its employees and the wider community.

Aerial Photo of Jackfield taken in summer 1948 showing a wealth of detail: notice the scale of the Maw's Tile Works in the foreground and the former tennis court on the right.

The footpath soon turns into Ferry Road with an example of a solidly built terrace of company housing on the right hand side.

7 The road exits into an open area in front of *The Boat Inn*, one of only three surviving pubs from the twenty three that Jackfield once boasted! It seems likely that it acquired so many because the village grew up in the 18C and the work of bargees and bow haulers, not to mention that of colliers and ironworkers, was thirsty work indeed!

Like many such establishments in the Gorge, *The Boat Inn* probably served as an illegal brewhouse and brothel long before it was licensed as a pub in 1840. It was originally part of a row of cottages, some of which have since been demolished. Its name derives from the ferry boat which used to operate here, particularly to take workers to and from the Coalport China Works on the north side of the river, before the Memorial footbridge was built in 1922. Today, the painting on the outside wall of the pub has been changed from that of the ferry, to one of the Severn trows, robust and elegant sailing vessels that plied their trade up and down the river. Indeed, in the upstairs living room is a huge 'floating' beam, reputedly the mast of one such trow.

ON CHRISTMAS EVE 1993

That evening the river rose so high that Half Moon' customers had to use stepping stones across the patio at the front in order to get to the bar, but the landlord continued to serve. Meanwhile, **The Boat Inn** had closed. Being that much lower down, water had entered the bar. On Boxing Day, the landlord of The Boat was impelled to order an unusual visitor from his garden: a canoeist!

Being low ground, next to the river, the pub has been flooded many times throughout its history, and when it is, the high flood marks have been faithfully recorded on an outside door of the building for all to see (formerly the marks were on the inside of the door in the bar). They make interesting reading with the very highest mark being as recent as November 1st 2000. Little wonder, therefore, that the pub often advertises itself as:

'The **Boat Inn** *at Jackfield, near the river Severn - and occasionally in it!'*

The area in the vicinity of the *Boat Inn* and at the back is known as the Tuckies. The river here flows very fast which made it suitable for the ferry to run, before the Jackfield & Coalport Memorial Bridge was built in 1922.

You can read more about the Ferry and the Memorial Bridge in walks nos 3 & 5

For other means of getting across the river see *'Coracles! Coracles!'* on page 52

Continue on the road with the pub garden on your right, until after a few metres to come to where the road swings round to the right. Do NOT go on the road but continue straight on until you come to a (somewhat muddy) path with a wooden kissing gate on your right leading into a field.

The Boat Inn, flooded in 1925

8 There is the option now of going through the kissing gate and taking a short-cut via a newly created path within the field on the right, known as Werps Field. This short-cut will bring you out to Step **11** on the route. If not taking the short-cut, continue straight on along the riverside path, passing another tall hummock on the left made by the dumping of yet more tile waste from Maw's. Continue on this riverside path until you come to a gate and stile.

> Werps Field (sometimes called *Boat Inn Field*) is an area of traditional meadow. 'Werp' is a word from which wharf is possibly derived, meaning at its simplest, a river embankment. The word has also been suggested to derive from the 'warping' of the currents of the river in the vicinity. The Trust manages the field as a wildflower grassland where species such as cowslip and common spotted orchid will thrive. The surrounding hedgerows and scrub habitat are also invaluable for butterflies and birds.

Some 80 metres downriver, you may notice that the path is 'brick-lined' in places. Shortly, on the right, there is a gap leading into a cleared area with a low brick retaining wall within the scrub woodland.

General
Gordon of
Khartoum

> These signs of brickwork are all that remains for the most part of The Werps district of Jackfield. From the 19C until the mid-20C there were some fifteen cottages and gardens here, built to form another of Jackfield's three 'Squares'. There was also a pub, formerly *The Werps Inn*, but renamed in 1885 as *The General Gordon* after the heroic - but ultimately vain - exploits of Major General Charles George Gordon who was killed in that year at Khartoum in Egypt. His heroism affected the national consciousness and many pubs were renamed overnight.

> The Werps district was particularly noted for its boat-building (there was a yard here) including that of coracles. The houses and pub were demolished in the 1950s as part of 'slum clearance' and with it another historic part of Jackfield disappeared forever.

9 Continue on the riverside path until you come to a gate. Pass through the kissing gate into the meadow. The path more or less follows the river for about 350 metres.

The General Gordon Inn (formerly The Werps Inn)
with licensee Henry Potts and family c 1900

ABOVE: *Coalport by H.Clements, 1884. William Reynolds huge warehouse straddling the canal can be seen, as well as Coalport Bridge, and a Toll House for barges on the right hand side*

BELOW: *Contemporary view of Coalport Bridge*

From here you are rewarded with some exceptional views across the river to Coalport with its China Museum and distinctive bottle kilns, and also to the new Reynolds' Wharf development. Indeed, if you look hard at the far bank, you can still see the line of sandstone arches at the water's edge - all that remains of the wharves and an enormous warehouse spanning the old canal and extending out to the river, built by the 18C ironmaster, entrepreneur, and founder of Coalport, William Reynolds.

On this side of the riverbank there is a stretch of rocky beach (where more industrial tile and china waste was deposited) where, if you are lucky, you might catch glimpses of the herons and kingfishers that occupy the river.

The view downriver is particularly pleasing, taking in the graceful span of the Coalport Bridge, formerly called the Preens Eddy Bridge when it was built of wood with stone abutments. (The nearby pub is called *The Woodbridge Inn*).

For more information on Coalport Bridge see walk no 3 Page 46

Continue along the rough, unmarked and somewhat muddy path which heads up across the field towards a power line. Just before this crosses the hedge on the hillside, you will find a kissing gate. Pause for a moment to turn round and look upstream. You will find a marvellous view of Ironbridge with the Wrekin behind.

10 Pass through the kissing gate onto the Severn Valley Way, where you should turn right.

The Severn Valley Way, now a major recreational route for walkers and cyclists, follows the line of the old Severn Valley Railway (SVR). Constructed from Hartlebury Junction, south of Kidderminster, following the line of the river to Shrewsbury, the SVR was opened in 1862 and became part of the Great Western Railway in 1872. It survived for the better part of a hundred years before closing - as with so many other lines in Britain - in the early 1960s.

Continue on the walk until you arrive at an interpretive board on the right (in front of the Werps Field which you passed earlier, lower down) and with a stile on your left.

11 The stile on the left leads into the woodland known as Preenshead, also managed by Severn Gorge Countryside Trust

Hazel catkins, traditional coppice species

Preenshead, although ancient semi-natural woodland in origin, appears to comprise stands that have grown since extensive felling in the 1940s. Most of the woodland is a mixture of ash, hazel, birch and young elm. Alder occupies some of the wetter areas. Although there is some access into the woodland, there is, unfortunately, no logical or comfortable circular route across the centre bringing you back onto the Severn Valley Way. As a small diversion, however, you may wish to explore this woodland.

12 The Severn Valley Way soon passes over a bridge which allows a road below to pass under the old railway line. There are steps down here which you should take, bringing you to what is called The Tuckies Road, serving the old community of The Tuckies.

Railway companies rarely went to the expense of building bridges unless they had to. The bridge here, the most notable and expensive example along the Gorge stretch of the SVR, is an indication of just how important the Tuckies Road used to be. It served The Tuckies community of perhaps a dozen houses (almost all gone) and a busy farm (no longer functioning) and connected with a main path through Corbett's Dingle to Broseley. Workers from there used this as their main route to get to and from work at Coalport China Works on the north side of the river.

Walk up the Tuckies Road for about 80 metres.

13 A private track off to the right serves The Tuckies house, the oldest and possibly most interesting house of any size within the Gorge:

The building was certainly there as a half-timbered house in 1667 with much of the construction using a mellow grey sandstone from nearby Corbett's Dingle. The Tuckies is a building of great interest historically. During the 1750s it was the home of Archibald Cochrane, 9th Earl of Dundonald, attributed as the inventor and developer of tar-oil distillation. In the latter part of that century it became home to the ironmaster, William Reynolds, perhaps the most visionary and enterprising of the 18C Gorge industrialists who was also responsible for the nearby 'new town' of Coalport. Towards the end of the 18C he planned (with Dundonald) a large chemical works, although this was never built.

Reynolds was responsible for renovating The Tuckies, including the erection of a fine cast iron verandah on the front of the building, offering wonderful views out and the opportunity to oversee the construction of his Coalport enterprise. In the 1850s the house was divided into three separate dwellings and the veranda subsequently removed. One of the dwellings still contains a magnificent staircase, constructed during the Geogian extension, with two enormous solid oak mitred heads on the newel post They can be lifted off - removed like a man's head off his shoulders!

The Tuckies House with Maw's Tile Works' circular reservoir in a field to the left

In the field in front of The Tuckies house is a curious circular brick-built structure, visible from the Severn Valley Way and the Tuckies Road. It was a purpose-built reservoir for the nearby decorative tile manufacturer, Maw & Co. From their factory below, they had a good view of the float mechanism which automatically indicated the water levels in the reservoir. The water was used for mixing clay to make slip.

Continue on for another 20 metres where the road comes to a Y-junction. Our walk takes us off to the right.

The left fork soon encounters a 5-barred gate and leads into Corbett's Dingle, a charming walk with a stream and old quarried sandstone faces running much of its length. It eventually leads to Coneybury Farm and Broseley and historically provided the main route for workers to and from their employment at the China Works in Coalport. The path is apt to get very muddy, especially in winter, but you may wish to explore this now or in the future.

14 Walk up the right hand fork of the Y. You will come to the Tuckies Farm buildings, now a private dwelling. The track you are on passes between the farmhouse and old byres and stables and thence to the back of The Tuckies house where a

WORKING AT THE TILERIES

"On Saturdays and holidays I used to help on the milk round, but in 1924 when I left school there wasn't a job for me there, so I went to the Wallace Tileries and worked as a surface labourer, pushing the tubs from the bank on to the top of the incline down to the works. As you had to be over sixteen to work underground, we were nearly all lads on the top. We'd have to be at work for 6am when the miners went down and you'd see them with their paraffin lamps and candles giving their checks in to the banksman before going down.

Although there was a certain amount of clay that had to be got out each day, there was only one shift and it finished at 2pm, when the miners came up. Then, to make up my money, I'd have to go down to the tileries and help Walter Griffiths sort the tiles as they came out of the kilns or perhaps barrow the coal round. My pay for five days a week and four hours on Saturday morning was twelve shillings and sixpence [12/6d].

The highest paid job at the works were the press-men and the hand-made tilers who got fifteen shillings [15s] a week. Sorters wore leather aprons and special leather palms to protect the hands from blisters through sorting thousands of tiles a week. The tiles would be carried out of the kiln in bundles called "burns", and put on edge on a long wooden bench. Then each one would be tapped on the end of the bench and if it stayed whole, it was put on a flat barrow to go to the stack. If it broke, it fell on to a big pile of tiles which I'd have to shovel into a barrow and take across the yard to the tip. All the roads round Jackfield were surfaced with broken roofing tiles! The most common illness was asthma brought on by the dust in the kilns, so most of the sorters smoked clay pipes to 'filter the air'."

1902 map showing Wallace Tileries in relation to Maw's, Severn Valley Railway, River Severn and The Boat Inn

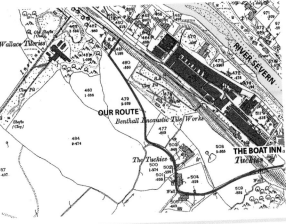

FOOTBALL AT CORONATION FIELD
EARLY DECADES
OF 20C

They used to like a good game of football in Jackfield. Most of the tileries had their own teams, but the top one in the village was the 'Jackfield Excelsiors'. They were sponsored by Mr Price-Jones who owned the Excelsior Roofing Tile Works at Coalford. They had various headquarters including **The Severn Trow**, then later the **The Black Swan**, but best known was 'The Boat' where they'd change into their red and white strip before running up to Maw's Coronation Field.

Many of the young lads working in Jackfield used to play football in their breaks on the Dial Meadow which is the field next to where the Wallace Pit was. Someone would bring a ball made from a pig's bladder, but occasionally we'd try to invite one of the manager's children who'd bring a real leather football. These were a real luxury, but the poorer kids - whose mothers had bought them clogs because they were cheaper - weren't allowed to play, in case they burst the ball!

very good view of the restored half-timbered dwelling is to be had. The track then goes past a modern dwelling and ends in a field gate with a kissing gate to the side leading to fields beyond.

15 Pass through the kissing gate and continue along the unmarked path through the fields ahead at approximately 45 degrees to the hedge on your right. The path is apt to get very muddy, especially in winter and you may wish to retrace your steps to the Severn Valley Way and continue your walk back to Jackfield Tile Museum that way.

If you pause after a 100 metres or so and look back, you will glimpse on the horizon a very old farm, Woodhouse Farm, parts of which are believed to go back to the 15C. Below the farm and over to the left of where you are standing there used to be an extensive tilery called the Wallace Tilery and above it a clay pit. There was also a long inclined plane for moving clay down to the works and a connection to the railways sidings at nearby Maw's for the transportation of finished tiles.

The enterprise like many others in the area lasted only for about fifty years, from 1890-1940, but during that time played an important part in the local economy, employing many men. Today, as you walk across the quiet fields, nothing but the smallest clues remain to intimate at the once noisy industrial past that marked this particular spot.

Continue following the track through the fields, bearing right to the bottom far end corner, where there is a gate and kissin gate, and a dozen steps leading down onto the Severn Valley Way.

The last field before the gate and the kissing gate, formerly known as Coronation Field, was the sports field for Jackfield School, but a bigger field

TONY MUGRIDGE:
Last of the Itinerant Brickmakers

In his 13 acre woodland, in the Ashtree district of Jackfield, Tony Mugridge uses local clay, already mined and brought to the surface from previous centuries, to make specialist hand-made bricks. He has developed his own kilns and brick-mould equipment and now has the proud distinction of being one of the last of the itinerant brickmakers in the UK.

Tony Mugridge with his wooden work shed comprised of part of Jackfield's former railway 'Halt'.

Even though bricks were being used by wealthier individuals in the 17C, the great age for brickmaking was throughout the 18C when the material increasingly came to replace timber-framing. Bricks constitute the very earliest manufactured product from natural materials rather than wrought from them, and because of the abundance of readily available clays in Jackfield, both its pottery industry and its brick and roof tile industry grew up from early times. Many of the early brick buildings were made from bricks which were hand-made on site where the travelling brickmaker might be contracted for a period from months to a couple years, say, before moving on to his next job. His equipment was always basic and portable.

Itinerant and country brickmakers have always been rural craftsmen as integral to the rural economy as those involved in ironworking, or the greenwood crafts, such as coppice workers. Indeed, small country brickmakers traditionally worked for the three seasons of spring, summer and autumn, whilst they coppiced during the winter months. Rather than using constructed kilns, many of those earlier brickmakers fired their products in clamps using coppiced materials for ease, cheapness and reliability.

Today, it is not only the needs of the conservation industry which require specialist hand-made bricks such as those made by Tony Mugridge, but a recognition that if we are to take seriously the issue of the rural economy we need to support and invest in traditional craft industries. To reassert the value of local distinctiveness is just one aspect of the debate over sustainability There are many others, but using local materials where available to provide services and products for local or regional needs is seen as desirable, rather than the environmental costs of transporting such materials from distant places of the country or globe.

Sample of hand-made bricks

in the shadow of Woodhouse Farm is where the local lads traditionally played their football in the first half of the 20C.

Just down from the dozen steps, on the opposite side of the road, is where a timbered hut and platform used to comprise the 'Jackfield Halt'. The village never had its own proper railway station, and when the 'Halt' became unusable due to the infamous landslip in April 1952, the new position for the 'Halt' was established further down line near the Tuckies Bridge, above *The Boat Inn.*

16 Turn left after the steps back along the Severn Valley Way.

The scrub woodland nearby is privately owned and shows a great deal of disturbance due to past clay mining and processing. Much of the land consists of clay spoil heaps, rejected material from a previous age but which nonetheless the present owner has put to a traditional and distinctive use - hand-made bricks for conservation and other customised work.

You will soon come to the section of Jackfield's famous 'temporary' wooden road laid over the bed of the former railway.

When in April 1983 the old Salthouse Road below, finally gave up the ghost by sliding into the river along with the sewer, gas and water mains, the County Council were forced to use the bed of the old railway as the new adopted road to allow vehicular access to that part of the village. That adopted road, too, began to distort and buckle, being on unstable ground, and use of steel-linked rafts of timber was used as some sort of solution. It requires regular maintenance, but, until perhaps one day a longer term solution can be found, it serves.

Continue on down the road to Jackfield Tile Museum and your starting point. Alternatively, you may wish to retrace your steps a little to explore Maw's Craft Centre where there is also a café.

'Wooden Road' (known locally as the 'Bumpy Boards') with main sewer above ground and view of St Mary's Spire, Jackfield

Coalport to The Hay Inclined Plane to Haywood Pastures to Silkin Way

This delightful country walk is a real pleasure all year round. Haywood has the benefit of a south-facing aspect and the open meadow land through which the walk passes is often bathed in glorious sunshine. The walk encompasses the land of the former **Hay Farm**, owned by the **Darby family** in the 18C. The initial woodland ride gives way to grassland, passes on to the historic **Hay Inclined Plane** with the remains of its engine house and chimney. The walk then traverses three traditionally-managed fields of grassland, the first of which is an old **anthill meadow**, reminiscent of earlier days and **now increasingly rare**. A bench and viewpoint at the mid-point of the walk provide spectacular views of the Severn Gorge in both directions. The walk concludes via the **Silkin Way**, today a local long-distance footpath and cycleway which runs along the bed of the **old branch line of the London & North Western Railway**.

 Accessibility: There are frequent muddy stretches to this walk and boots are recommended all year round. There is a reasonably steep climb at the beginning of the walk and three kissing gates to negotiate. *Note:* from April to November the fields are stocked with a small herd of grazing cattle, which can be inquisitive.

 Key Features: Nature, viewpoints, industrial and social history
Length & Time: 2½ km about 1-1¼ hours

 Public Transport: Buses to Coalport

 Refreshments: Shakespeare Inn (Coalport), The Brewery Inn (Coalport), The Boat Inn (Jackfield).

 Toilets: Coalport China Museum, John Rose Building (Youth Hostel)

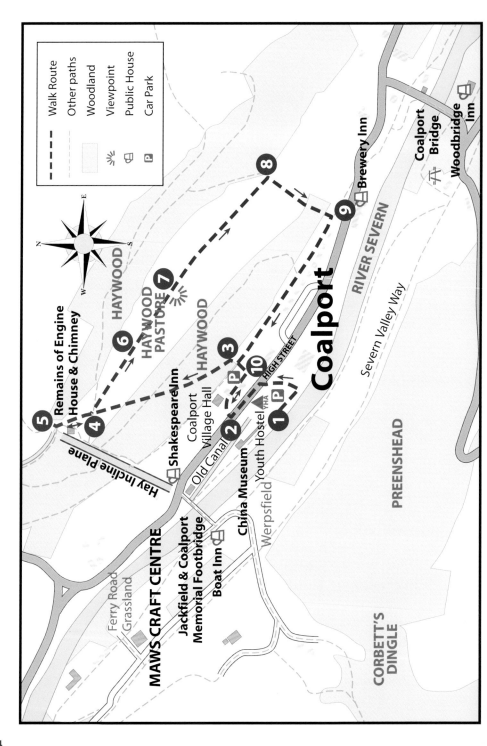

Coalport

RIVER SEVERN

Severn Valley Way

PREENSHEAD

CORBETT'S DINGLE

Woodbridge Inn

Coalport Bridge

Brewery Inn

HIGH STREET

HAYWOOD

HAYWOOD PASTURE

HAYWOOD

Remains of Engine House & Chimney

Hay Incline Plane

Shakespeare Inn

Coalport Village Hall

Old Canal

China Museum

Werpsfield Youth Hostel

Jackfield & Coalport Memorial Footbridge

Boat Inn

MAWS CRAFT CENTRE

Ferry Road Grassland

Legend

- Walk Route
- Other paths
- Woodland
- Viewpoint
- Public House
- Car Park

1

Starting at the Coalport China Museum car park, the John Rose Building, a rectangular building with cast-iron windows, is of historical interest.

John Rose, awarded a Society of Arts gold medal for his invention of lead-free glazes in 1820 but the mandatory use of such glazes took another 130 years to come into force!

John Rose established his pottery on this site as the Coalport China Manufactory in 1795. Having served an apprenticeship in nearby Caughly and set up a modest factory in Jackfield on the south side of the river, Rose and partner, Edward Blakeway, decided to move to this site to take advantage of the momentous changes being instigated by William Reynolds in the creation of his 'new town' of Coalport. Rose was a talented potter and the production of china here became hugely successful. His original factory was purpose-built, designed to house a workforce of a hundred under one roof, and indicates how the Industrial Revolution was beginning to transform the scale of industry from domestic workshop to large factory. In 1814 John Rose took over his brother's china business on the other side of the canal, and in the process formed a single business on this site which prospered throughout the 19C. China manufacture finally came to an end here in 1926, although Coalport china is still made in the Potteries today. Notice how many windows there are on the top floor of the building where the meticulous work of painting and gilding the china took place, requiring well-lit work rooms. The building was subsequently put to other uses and acquired its present use as a Youth Hostel in 1996.

Both the technological achievement of the nearby Hay Inclined Plane and the proximity of the river Severn go some way to explaining the success of china production at Coalport. The Inclined Plane could get raw materials and finished goods in and out of the Coalport basin very quickly and the River Severn, later the railway network, would carry goods throughout the country and beyond to international markets.

Walk out of the car park and turn left into Coalport High Street.

A private dwelling, tucked back off the road on the right, opposite the front of the John Rose Building, is Rose Cottage. John Rose lived here for a while in the 19C, and certainly didn't have far to go to work!

2 Continue on down the road for about 50 metres until you come to a sign post indicating right to Coalport Village Hall. Turn right here in front of the new Village Hall and subsequently follow the path through the car park to the Silkin Way.

The car park area used to be a storage area for the weathering of china clay and for feldspar used in the manufacturing process. It was also a place where animal bones were brought, used to make the bone china, and where children would sometimes play.

For 'The Case of the Disappearing Tea Services'
See Page 49

3 Cross over the Silkin Way to the gate opposite. Pass through this and turn sharp left up a broad woodland ride.

Animal Bones

"We used to play here often. One of the jobs the workers at the China Factory had to do was to strip the fat from the stacked-up piles of animal bones, before these went into the kiln to be used to make the bone china. People used to complain about the smoke from the factory and the reek and stench from the burning bones, but as children we never noticed. Well, children don't, do they? We didn't. We were too busy having a good time. When they'd put all the stripped fat into a container, we used to thrust our arms right in and squeeze it! When I tell people this story, they grimace. But we thought it was great fun!"

Haywood as a whole is an area of relatively young mixed woodland, intersected by a broad area of grassland. The woodland is dominated by a mix of larch, alder and birch.

Continue on up the ride until you come to a 5-barred gate and kissing gate. Pass through the gate and continue up towards the brick chimney through a contrasting landscape of open grassland and scrub. After about another 70 metres you will come to a marker post on your left.

Ringlet butterfly

4 There are several paths from this marker. We will be turning sharp right, taking the lower, less definite path through the grassland [**Consult Walk Map for the line of this path**] but first, as an interesting extension, our walk goes straight on up for another 100 metres or so to the top of the historic Hay Inclined Plane with the surviving remains of its engine house and chimney.

5 Pause for a moment here to look down on the rails of the Inclined Plane.

Late 18th/early 19C Hay Inclined Plane

Still considered one of Britain's foremost industrial monuments, the 305-metre long Hay Inclined Plane was an astonishing engineering achievement which linked the Shropshire Canal at Blist's Hill to the Coalport canal-river basin below. In this way goods and raw materials could be moved in a matter of minutes over a difference of levels of some 61 metres, equivalent to 27 conventional locks.

The Inclined Plane came into use in 1792, and employed a Heslop steam engine to haul up loaded tub boats. It continued to work for over a hundred years, a wonderful testimony to the quality of its design and was absolutely instrumental in securing William Reynolds' vision for his 'new town' of Coalport. Within two years of the incline starting operations, wharves, workshops, warehouses and rows of workers' houses had grown up and the area of the canal-river interchange was being referred to as 'Coalport'.

The Hay Inclined Plane ceased operations in 1894, with final closure in 1907.

Now retrace your steps back to the marker post below and thence along the path through the meadow/scrub as indicated earlier. The area you are walking through is sometimes referred to 'anthill meadow'.

Such invertebrates, interesting and valuable in their own right, also provide a rich source of food for a number of bird species. The ants most in abundance here are yellow meadow ants. If you walk this stretch cautiously, you may well notice a number of bird species feeding or foraging in the adjacent rambling scrub, such as greenfinch, redwing in winter, and the insectivorous goldcrest.

However, most likely to be seen are green woodpeckers which feed extensively on ants and find such sources here irresistible.

Today, management of the mixed habitats that Haywood offers - woodland, hedge, scrub, meadow - is significantly increasing the wildlife value of the area. The first step has been to reduce the number of cattle grazing the land. Grazing animals are a remarkable management tool in their own right - selectively eating plants, turning over nutrients and providing continuous fertilisation without recourse to artificial fertilizers (manure itself is a rich habitat, which over-use of animal 'worming' chemicals can seriously damage). However, over-grazing reduces habitat diversity, and the aim therefore is to strike an appropriate balance. In this anthill meadow every attempt is made to preserve the habitat (for example, keeping grass cropped to levels sufficient to maintain temperatures ideal for ants!), to encourage young regenerating scrub, coppice older scrub, and to plant and protect young scrub from grazing cattle. In this way, butterflies and moths increase, as do other invertebrates, and those species that predate them.

Green Woodpecker

6 Pass through the wooden gate into a large sloping meadow. After a few metres if you look up to the left, you will spot a bench higher in the field. Make for this where you will be rewarded with a rest and magnificent views of the whole of this stretch of the Severn Gorge.

The woodland on the opposite side of the valley is the ash-dominated Preenshead and Corbett's Dingle. Just to the right of that you can make out The Tuckies, reputedly the oldest house of any size within the Gorge which became the home of the ironmaster William Reynolds. The views off to the left (the east) are just as splendid with Sutton Maddock church clearly visible.

The grassland all about you is part of the original Hay Farm, owned by the Darby family in the 18C. The farm provided a home, but was also used commercially, especially as the means of rearing the hundreds of horses which the Darbys used in their industrial enterprises The farm used to extend right down to the river, as well as up and beyond, but much of the former open pasture became woodland when it was planted during the 1960s by Telford Development Corporation.

When you have taken in enough of the views, continue on the path through the field, passing through into another field and eventually to the gate in the middle of the hedge.

7 Do not proceed into the last meadow but turn sharp right and follow the fence down to another kissing gate in the corner of the field **[Consult the map for the line of the path]**. The area here can be very muddy. Pass through the gate and subsequently down a pleasant track, flanked by tall hedges, to meet the Silkin Way.

Opposite this point, on the other side of the road, is *The Brewery Inn*. Built in the 1850s, it is so called because it was licensed to brew ale on its premises (unlike the many illegal brewhouses).

The pub was owned by the Coalport China Works and formed part of a well-built terrace of workers' cottages. The pub reputedly had a history of supplying beer for a while to other local pubs such as *The Shakespeare Inn* in Coalport by means of

The Brewery Inn

the canal which formerly ran at the back of the pub (there are surviving remains) and also to the *Boat Inn* in nearby Jackfield via the river. The barrels were loaded by means of a short incline from the canal to the river to be transported. There is a little beer garden at the back with fine views across the river.

8 Turn right down the Silkin Way and continue walking for about 350 metres until you come to the gap on the left (opposite a seat and gate on the other side of the Silkin Way) leading back to the car park to the side of the new Village Hall from where you came earlier.

The Silkin Way is a local long-distance footpath and cycleway, linking the north and south ends of the new town of Telford, a distance of some 14 miles. The route was established along the former branch line of the London & North Western Railway (LNWR) which closed in 1952 (freight ten years later) but which for more than a hundred years played such a vital part in the life of the local community.

9 From the Village Hall car park return to the High Street and thence to the China Museum car park and the John Rose Building.

MEMORIES OF A COALPORT RAILWAYMAN'S SON

"My father was a porter-signalman for the London &
North Western Railway (LNWR). He was a Potter (meaning
he came from the Potteries) and started to work at
Coalport in about 1938 after a couple of years at Madeley
Station. The job at Coalport was a promotion to
signalman and after a while they found him this railway
cottage to live in so that he didn't have to commute from
Madeley. These cottages are interesting in themselves
because they look identical but aren't. This one was
probably built for a station foreman and has a living room
which is 12 feet square, whereas next door must have been
built for a lower rank and his family as the living room there
is only 10 feet 6 inches square. Although he worked pretty
well all his life on the railways, my father was actually a very
good amateur footballer and Port Vale wanted to sign him professionally. His father
wouldn't hear of it, told him to get a job on the railways which was a job for life, because
in those days there was no security or money in being a footballer(!)"

*Bert (Bob) Banks with sons
outside Coalport East
Station in 1948*

Gradient of the Line out of Coalport

"One of the most remarkable things about the LNWR line out of Coalport was the gradient
of 1in 40, sharpening to 1 in 32 near Blists Hill. When you think that 1 in 100 was probably
the norm for a main line, you can imagine the effort in getting up that hill out of the
village. They used to struggle in wet weather, and if there was a really large freight load,
they might have as many as three engines on - two at the front and one at the rear. Once,
I remember getting on a train after my father had finished his shift. He had time to wash,
shave and change into 'civvies', then wheel his bike up to Madeley and still he overtook us.
It was so wet that we had taken more than half an hour just getting to the first rise. We
were standing there, wheels spinning, when he overtook us."

The Coalport "Dodger"

"The "Dodger" was so-called because it was the train that ran up and down the LNWR
branch line between Wellington and Coalport, a journey time of only forty minutes.
Farmers moved livestock to market, and people availed themselves of the greater
shopping and social opportunities in Madeley, Oakengates and Wellington. Many of the
teenagers from Madeley used the Dodger for their day out. They'd catch the train down
to Coalport, then walk or ride down a private road to Sweneye Cliffe. There was a sandy
stretch along the river, known as 'Sandy Banks', where it was safe to paddle. Afterwards,
they'd have a picnic, before getting the train back home to Madeley."

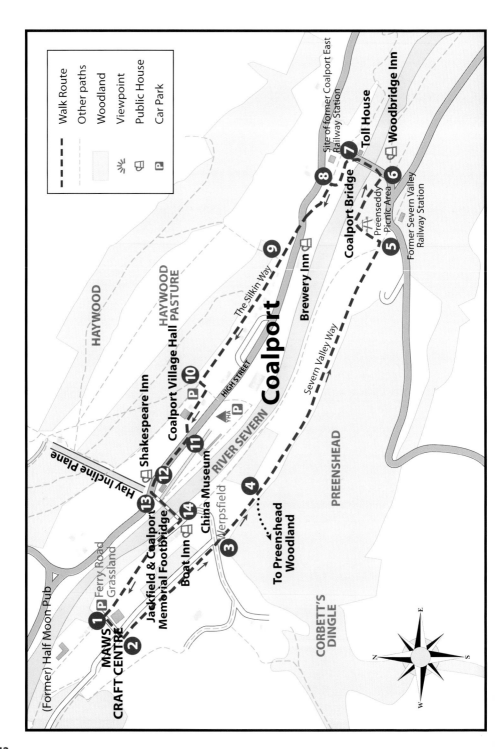

Legend

- – – Walk Route
- - - Other paths
- Woodland
- ☆ Viewpoint
- ⊟ Public House
- ℗ Car Park

Coalport

HAYWOOD

HAYWOOD PASTURE

The Silkin Way

RIVER SEVERN

PREENSHEAD

Severn Valley Way

CORBETT'S DINGLE

Hay Incline Plane

HIGH STREET

Shakespeare Inn

Coalport Village Hall

China Museum

Werpsfield

Boat Inn

Jackfield & Coalport Memorial Footbridge

Ferry Road Grassland

MAWS CRAFT CENTRE

(Former) Half Moon Pub

To Preenshead Woodland

Brewery Inn

Coalport Bridge

Toll House

Woodbridge Inn

Preenseddy Picnic Area

Former Severn Valley Railway Station

Site of former Coalport East Railway Station

① ② ③ ④ ⑤ ⑥ ⑦ ⑧ ⑨ ⑩ ⑪ ⑫ ⑬ ⑭

Maw's Craft Centre to The Severn Valley Way to Coalport Bridge to Silkin Way to the Memorial Bridge

Starting from Maw's Craft Centre which occupies some of the surviving buildings of the **Maw's Tile Works**, this historic walk begins by travelling down the line of the **former Severn Valley Railway**, from where there is a view of **The Tuckies**, the oldest house of any size in the Gorge, with lovely views also across the river to Coalport. The walk crosses the **Coalport Bridge**, a late 18C/early 19C cast iron bridge still carrying vehicles, thence drops down to river level, before gently inclining along the **Silkin Way**, established on the bed of the other railway that Coalport once boasted, the **London & North Western Railway (LNWR)**. The walk continues down a short section of the High Street, passes the impressive Hay Inclined Plane and the nearby Tar Tunnel, and then crosses the **Jackfield & Coalport Memorial Footbridge**.

🏃 **Accessibility:** There can be some muddy sections along this walk and boots or stout footwear are recommended. The walk is largely on the level, without stiles, but with steps up and down the Memorial Bridge, and around the picnic area of Preenseddy. Care is needed along the short section of Coalport High Street – children will need to be supervised.

🔆 **Key Features:** Industrial and social history, archeology, views, nature

🕐 **Length & Time:** 3½ km about 1½-1¾ hours

🚌 **Public Transport:** Buses to Jackfield and Coalport

🍺 **Refreshments:** Maw's Craft Centre, The Woodbridge Inn, The Brewery Inn, The Shakespeare Inn, The Boat Inn.

🚻 **Toilets:** The China Museum, Coalport Youth Hostel, Maw's Craft Centre

1 Maw's Craft Centre (car park nearby) is the starting point for this walk and is well worth a visit either now or at the end of the walk. The Centre utilises a number of the surviving buildings of what was once the largest decorative tile manufacturer in the world.

It is difficult, even from the extensive surviving buildings, to get an idea of just how vast Maw & Co. was in its heyday. It dwarfed the surrounding village, had a workforce of many hundreds, and produced millions of tiles each year. Something of the sheer size and complexity of the operations can be gauged from the aerial photograph of Jackfield taken in 1948 *(Page 23)*

The preserved tiled entrance to the former Maw's Tile Works now Maw's Craft Centre

More information about Maw & Co. Can be obtained from Walk no 1 on Page 14

With Maw's frontage on your left, cross the road ahead and walk up the slope towards the Severn Valley Way.

2 Turn left onto the Severn Valley Way and continue straight on.

The path you are now on is a major recreational route for walkers and cyclists, built along the bed of the Severn Valley Railway (SVR) which was opened in 1862 and closed a hundred years later.

After about 200 metres a large house (3 dwellings nowadays) called 'The Tuckies' comes into view on the right hand side across a field which usually has horses and ponies grazing.

The Tuckies is the oldest and arguably the most interesting house of any size within the Gorge, dating from at least 1667.

Walk no 1 is a delightful walk which passes close to The Tuckies houses and the history of the building is considered in much more detail on Page 21

A further 100 metres on and you come to a bridge, allowing The Tuckies Road to pass beneath the railway.

3 Pause for a moment here.

> If you move to the left hand side of the bridge, and then glance over to the right of the road below, you will see a pair of modern cottages. A pub called The Duke of Wellington used to be on that site along with its bowling green. On the left of the road and much nearer the river, you can make out the roofs of a number of buildings, including *The Boat Inn,* a still thriving establishment.

Carry on for another 150 metres until you come to a field on your left with an interpretive board and a stile opposite leading into woodland on your right.

4 Pause for a moment, perhaps taking the opportunity to read the interpretive board.

> The field below the interpretive board is Werps Field (sometimes called *Boat Inn* Field) now a traditional meadow.

> Just to the right of Werps Field is an area of scrub woodland. Here the old district of the Werps used to comprise many cottages and gardens and a pub called *The Werps Inn*, later renamed *The General Gordon*. The buildings were demolished and the area cleared in the 1950s as part of a 'slum clearance' programme.

Common spotted orchid

> The stile on the right hand side of the path leads into Preenshead, an area of formerly ancient woodland. It is now comprised of relatively young stands of ash, hazel, birch and elm due to an extensive programme of felling in the 1940s. The woodland is also managed by Severn Gorge Countryside Trust. but there is, unfortunately, no logical or comfortable circular route across the centre bringing you back onto the Severn Valley Way. However, you may wish to explore Preenshead for a little while as a diversion.

The remainder of this section of the walk down the Severn Valley Way is a pleasant stroll of about half a mile, with woodland to the right, and scrub to the left but occasionally allowing splendid glimpses across the river to the village of Coalport.

There are distinctive remains of its china industry, now a major museum site. At the end of the former line, the path turns sharp left.

5 A few metres after the sharp left turn, you may notice a gate, and, tucked back, a black and white, half-timbered cottage and garden with the unusual name of Ward's Tyning. It is notable as possibly one of the oldest cottages in the Gorge. The path continues down for a while, then curves round to the right, through Preenseddy picnic area, former meadow land, and thence up some steps to the road. Coalport Bridge is on your left and the Woodbridge Inn more or less straight over the road.

6 Before you turn left over the bridge, look to the right.

Behind you, tucked back but clearly visible, is the former Great Western Railway Station of the Severn Valley Railway, one of two railway stations that Coalport once boasted. The building is a private dwelling now. In the garden is a restored GWR coach.

Walk over the Coalport Bridge with the former toll house on the right hand side.

The Woodbridge pub gives a clue to the history of Coalport Bridge. It was formerly called the Preens Eddy Bridge when it was built of wood with stone abutments The bridge was completed and opened in the spring of 1780 (rather earlier than the famous Iron Bridge just two miles upstream which opened for traffic on 1st January 1781) but was severely damaged in the great floods of February 1795. Repairs using iron transformed the timber bridge into a hybrid supported by three cast iron ribs. This arrangement was short-lived, however, as the central rib cracked in 1817, requiring two more iron ribs for strengthening, completing the structure as it stands today.

The Woodbridge Inn

Coalport bridge remains the only cast iron bridge which still carries vehicular traffic. In 2004/5 it underwent major renovation and strengthening.

7 On the other side of the bridge, look out for a wooden 5-barred gate on your left and a sign marked to the 'Silkin Way'. Follow the sign, walking down the gently sloping path ahead of you.

MISS GREEN, THE TOLLKEEPER'S DAUGHTER

"I believe the tolls on the Coalport Bridge were discontinued sometimes in the 1920s or 1930s but the single barrier gate was still there in the late 1940s because I remember it when I was lad. Even after they had discontinued the tolls, and after the tollkeeper had died, his daughter, Miss Green, continued to live in the cottage. She was a diminutive woman. She kept a sort of shop at the tollhouse, fetched a few staple items, such as cigarettes and sweets from Ironbridge, for the convenience of the local people. The shop had a stable door, the lower half with a ledge which operated as the counter, and she was so short that her head scarcely came above the top of the counter! The tollhouse in those days had a bay window which gave her a good view of traffic approaching the bridge. For years after the tolls had finished, if she didn't like the look of some lorry or other heavy load intending to cross, she'd rush out of the cottage, draw the gate across the bridge and remonstrate with the driver of the vehicle she'd taken exception to. They usually backed off, thinking that she must be in the right, even though she hadn't the slightest authority to do what she did."

Former tollhouse, Coalport Bridge

The Silkin way starts here, a local long-distance footpath and cycleway linking the south and north ends of the new town of Telford. The route has been established along the bed of the former branch line of the London & North Western Railway (LNWR) which opened in June 1861 and closed in 1952 (freight 10 years later). For a hundred years the railway played a vital part in the life of the community. Unlike the GWR station, nothing remains of the LNWR station, but at the bottom, when you come to the T-junction, look to your right. This side of the 1995-reconstructed brick railway bridge is the site of that station.

8 Turn left at the T-junction, and after another 100 metres or so, take the right fork which winds behind the LNWR railway cottages, under the road bridge, before emerging to run parallel to Coalport High Street. When you come to a car park on your left, pause for a moment.

9 If you look left, on the other side of the road is a pub with an interesting history.

The Brewery Inn was built in the 1850s, owned by the China Works, and was so-called because it was licensed to brew ale on the premises – unlike the many illegal brewhouses in the area.

The history of *The Brewery Inn* is considered in more detail in Walk no 2 on Page 39

Continue on this straight stretch of the Silkin Way. The woodland and meadowland of Haywood is on your right offering opportunities for another splendid walk on another day *(Walk No 2).* You will come to a point along the path with another path off to the left. You can identify the point because opposite, on the right, is a wooden seat and gate leading into Haywood.

10 Take the left turn which passes behind, then through the car park of Coalport Village Hall, before exiting into the High Street.

See the story *'Animal Bones'* on Page 36

Coalport China Museum

Directly opposite is the Coalport China Museum with the John Rose Building, now a Youth Hostel, off to the left.

John Rose, a talented potter and inventor of lead-free glazes, was the first to establish a china works on this site at a time when William Reynolds was developing the area in the late 18C. The banks of the Reynolds' canal provided an ideal location for this type of manufactory, since coal could easily be transported from the coalfields via the canal, used to fire the kilns, whilst the proximity of the river Severn - later the railway system - provided the means of shipping the finished products to their markets, at home and abroad.

You can read more about John Rose in Walk no 5 Page 69

11 Turn right down Coalport High Street. Further down on the right you will come to *The Shakespeare Inn* and car park also on the right.

The Shakespeare Inn

The cleared space, now a car park, used to have on it a terrace of workers' cottages called Jug Row, due to the middle building being a pub called *The Jug & Bottle.* Both this pub and *The Shakespeare Inn* provided refreshment for the many workers in the area, not least those at Blist's Hill, and those working the Hay Inclined Plane just to the side of the pub, as well as for the china workers.

THE CASE OF THE DISAPPEARING TEA SERVICES

Early manufacturers were just as concerned about theft from places of work as today. They devised numerous deterrents. Some mine owners distinguished their mine candles from the usual tallow-coloured ones by the use of verdigris: any miner found burning green candles at home for personal use was sacked. The Coalbrookdale Company regularly issued dire threats of dismissal and/or fines for anyone found stealing from its coal stocks. But the management at the Coalport China Works in the early 20C had to employ the unusual crime-solving methods of the local constable "Bobby" Bowen when they suspected their warehouse women of stealing whole tea services.

It was alleged that quite a few women walked out of the factory gates rather 'stiff-limbed' with a dinner plate to their belly, another to their back, and two soup bowls in a certain place further up. Then, under their long skirts and coats, they hung cups, tied by their handles on long strings. If that wasn't enough, it is said they tied side plates to their thighs!

"Bobby" Bowen used to wait at the end of the Coalport Bridge, next to the Toll-house. When the women came through, he would stop them and lightly tap their fronts and backs. It is said that if there was a 'ringing' sound, he would arrest them, but if he heard a 'cracking' sound, he let them off!!

Postcript: It is probable that if they ever dredged the river Severn at Coalport, they'd bring up more china tea services than a museum curator could dream of! Suspecting they might be caught, many women extricated the items from their persons and disposed of them in the river!

12 Continue on past the pub, over the road bridge, to a turning off to the left and a few steps down. From there, you can view the restored section of the Coalport canal and, looking back, get a good view of the Hay Inclined Plane as it passes under the road.

The Hay Inclined Plane was an astonishing engineering feat, and continued to work for over a hundred years, moving goods and raw materials in a matter of minutes from the East Shropshire Canal at Blist's Hill down to the River Severn

Walk no 2 is a charming walk of about 1 hour which visits the remains of the Engine House and chimney of the Hay Inclined Plane. The history of the monument is considered in more detail in that walk on Page 37

Just to the side of the canal where you are standing is a sign and entrance to another remarkable construction, The Tar Tunnel. This was built by the industrialist and entrepreneur, William Reynolds, who, tunnelling for other purposes, caused a stream of tar to pour out of the side of the tunnel. This was exploited commercially, before ceasing to flow altogether nearly sixty years later!

You can learn more about the Tar Tunnel in Walk no 5 on Page 68

13 Now walk over the Jackfield & Coalport Memorial footbridge to the other side of the river.

The footbridge replaced the ferry in 1922 and immediately provided a safe, secure, and more convenient means of linking the two communities. It was especially important to the Jackfield workers who travelled each day to and from work at the Coalport China Works.

The story of the Bridge: 'A Most Useful, Unusual War Memorial' is on Page 68., told by a contemporary of the time

There was one other means of getting across the river in the days before the footbridge - by coracle! Sometimes the ferry wasn't operating, sometimes you just wanted to go by coracle! Some of the often-amusing exploits of coraclers (makers and users) are related below.

TOP: *Jackfield Ferry*
ABOVE: *Memorial Bridge*

See story: 'Coracles! Coracles!' Page 52

On the other side of the bridge you are met by a pleasant riverside area fronting a 19C pub, *The Boat Inn*.

The Boat Inn was originally part of a row of cottages, some of which have since been demolished. Its name derives from the ferry boat which used to operate here, and was formally licensed in 1840, although it had probably operated – like many such establish-

ments in the Gorge – as an illegal brewhouse and brothel long before that.

For more information on *The Boat Inn* see walk no 1 page 23

The Boat Inn today

14 From the bridge turn right up Ferry Road, past a solidly-built terrace of company houses on the left. Actually, just past the pub, the first house on the corner of the terrace used to be a shop with a flight of steps up by the side leading to Jackfield's Railway 'Halt' on the Severn Valley Railway. Past the housing, the road gives way to a path in the lee of the former tile factory of Maw & Co. On the right is a pleasant area of amenity grassland. You will soon notice ahead a rather strange chute emerging from the brick wall on your left.

The chute was designed to convey tile waste from the Maw's factory and to be at such a height that a horse and cart could fit conveniently beneath it.

The grassland to your right is actually comprised largely of huge quantities of ceramic tile waste, dumped there over a long period of time. The 'green' used to have a number of buildings on it – cottages, as well as the Maw's canteen known as the 'Mess Room'. This also doubled at times as the Village Hall and at one point as a temporary home for the Jackfield Brass Band, an institution of which the community is justly proud. The area even had a tennis court on it at one time.

Maw's waste chute

Continue up the path, past the grassland until you come back to your starting point at Maw's Craft Centre.

Jackfield Brass Band

To give it its present-day title, Jackfield Elcock Reisen Band is not the oldest brass band in the country, but it does have the unusual distinction of having played continuously without a break - despite two World Wars - since its founding. It started life as a Drum & Fife band in 1893, quickly turning to all-brass a couple of years later. Investing in a new set of instruments in 1926, for awhile it was referred to as a "silver" band, even as the 'Jackfield Prize Silver Band' on account of the many prizes it won over the years. It remains a source of great pride to the people of Jackfield and the Gorge, not

least for the quality of its musicianship and as an enduring institution in the life of the community. After so many 'homes' over the years - including the canteen or 'Mess Room' at the tile manufacturer, Maw's & Co, and the old 'Bake-House' near the former Tumbling Sailors public house in the Lloyds district, the band now has a secure home after it bought the Coalford Methodist Chapel in Jackfield in 1991.

Coracles! Coracles!

Coracles were always important in the Ironbridge Gorge (as elsewhere on other stretches of the Severn). The most famous family makers of this versatile little craft - one that you could pick up, put on your back, and carry where you wanted - was the Rogers family of Ironbridge. Several generations of coracle makers came to an end in 2004 with the death of Eustace Rogers. His father, Harry, is seen here demonstrating the paddling of a coracle in the bar of an Ironbridge pub for an early BBC publication called Country Magazine Television in about 1951.

CONTINUED OVERLEAF

Harry also offers a discourse on what coracles were used for:

"For generations, coracles have been our family job and we still make 'em. We use them still for lots of things, and some I'll tell you about, and some I won't. [Dead rabbit on table - bit of a giveaway.] They're the only craft that will stand up to Severn when she's in flood. Severn's always up to one of her tricks, but she's like a woman· you can read her if you study her aright."

Harry was quite a character. He had a pet fox, for example, which he walked on a lead round Ironbridge, or draped round his neck like a stole. It could be a bit disconcerting if you stopped to have a chat with him in the High Street, when the fox sleeping, or apparently long dead would suddenly open its eyes and stare at you!

Coracles were also used and made particularly in Jackfield, in the Werps district near **The Boat Inn**. One of the best known coraclers was Frank Poole (1883-1972) who after living for a number of years in Jackfield, moved across river to Coalport. [His uncle, William, was one of the ferrymen].His day job was as a qualified bricklayer and he worked much of the time on vital work in the pits. In his spare time he made coracles for his own use and for others. He fished with them, "mainly for eels and salmon, but eels were always considered the better treat". In Frank Poole's early days there was no Memorial Footbridge (built 1922), and if the ferry was laid up for any reason, the only way of getting across the river was either a long

walk around to the other side via the Coalport Bridge (Wood Bridge) or the Free Bridge. That's when a coracle came in particularly handy!

TOP: *Protrait of Frank Poole, 1904*
ABOVE: *Frank Poole's great Grandson with Eustace Rogers discussing the finer points of coracle making*

Another local resident, Norman Hudson, of that generation recalls:

"Most of the folk down that end of Jackfield had coracles or some even had boats. This is because when the river flooded, you couldn't get out by road. You'd see the boats tied up to the guttering and down-pipes on the houses, so people could climb out of their bedroom windows and row or paddle to work. Trouble was, the river level would go down just as quickly as it came up and you might see the gutter missing off a house where the weight of a dinghy had ripped it off, or even a coracle hanging high on a chimney!"

CONTINUED OVERLEAF

One notable Jackfield coracle user was a Mr Harrison who lived in the end house of the Ferry Road terrace next to **The Boat Inn**. He was especially adept with a coracle. They say the best technique is to turn the paddle in a figure of eight in the water and you sort of go along a bit from side to side. But if you don't do this, you end up going round and round in circles, or even tipping up and going for a surprise swim!

Norman Hudson recalls an amusing incident:

"One day a well-dressed gent in a bowler hat and carrying an umbrella was standing by the ferry stage looking very perplexed. After a few minutes, he caught the eye of Mr Harrison and asked what had happened to the ferry. Once he had been told - it may have been that the ferry was laid up because of the ferryman's ill-health - it became apparent there was a problem as the gentleman had a train to catch on the Coalport side and needed to get over the river post haste. He was willing to pay anyone who could take him. Mr Harrison said he could take him but as coracles were only really designed to take one person, the gentleman would need to sit very still whilst he was paddled across. The fare was agreed, and the gent sat as directed, very still. Mr Harrison then started to paddle the coracle across river. The two men began chatting. The gentleman explained that he came to Jackfield once a year to see Mr. Maw and always went to Coalport on the ferry before catching the train to Wellington. As he became a little more relaxed he rested his hands on the top of his brolly and

suddenly .. "Pop!". He'd pushed the spike straight through the bottom of the coracle. He was about to remove it when Mr Harrison, with a few choice words, and a restraining hand, told him to leave it right there or they'd both get a good soaking!

They made it to the Coalport side, and, after apologies and payment for both ride and repairs, our gentlemen made his way to the station."

Actually, though clearly designed for only one person, as with other forms of transport coracles were often used to carry a number of people in situations that must have severely tested the skills of the coracler. Frank Poole's grand-daughter, Moyra Dolman, recalls how her mother remembers regularly crossing the river in the family coracle with her one sister and Frank Poole and his wife and .. the dog, a Jack Russell, who at a certain distance from the Jackfield side had the disconcerting habit of leaping out to swim the remaining metres!

Mr Green opperating his coracle as a ferry between Minehole and The Wharf on the Jackfield side and houses on the opposite side.

Coalport Bridge to Silkin Way to Sutton Wood

This is a real gem of a walk through some delightful and little explored woodland. The start point is at the Woodbridge Inn, whose name betrays a time when **Coalport Bridge** was made largely of wood. The path descends to river level, past the site of the site of the **former Coalport East Station of the London & North Western Railway (LNWR)** and some old railway cottages, before ascending through the western part of Sutton Wood via a set of newly constructed steps. The walk then describes a loop within the verdant central part of **Sutton Wood** before returning homewards through another section of the woodland.

Accessibility: Boots or stout shoes are needed all year round for frequently muddy sections on this walk. There are some steep ascents and descents via constructed steps, with a number of convenient access gates and four conventional stiles. There is a small woodland pool near to the walk - children will need supervision.

Key Features: Ecology, natural history, some industrial heritage

Length & Time: About 4km – about 1¾-2 hours

Public Transport: Buses to Coalport

Refreshments: Woodbridge Inn, Brewery Inn

Toilets: Woodbridge Inn, Brewery Inn, Youth Hostel, China Museum.

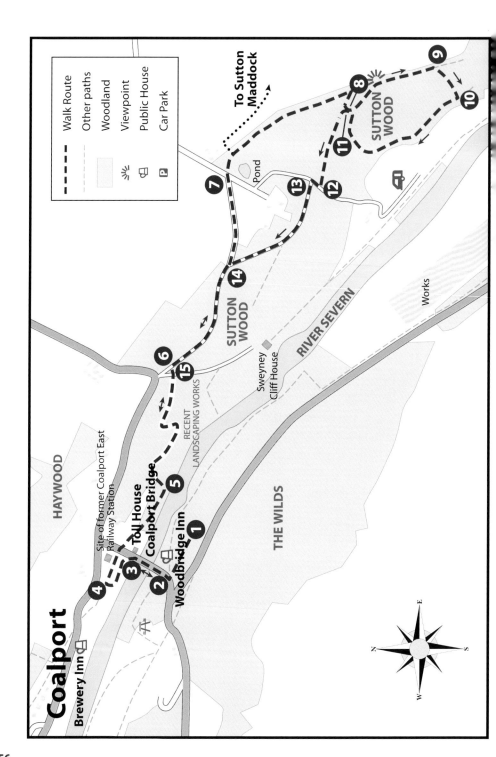

Coalport

Brewery Inn

Walk Route
Other paths
Woodland
Viewpoint
Public House
Car Park

HAYWOOD

Site of former Coalport East
Railway Station

Toll House
Coalport Bridge

Woodbridge Inn

RECENT
LANDSCAPING WORKS

SUTTON
WOOD

Sweyney
Cliff House

RIVER SEVERN

THE WILDS

Works

SUTTON
WOOD

Pond

To Sutton
Maddock

1 Starting at the *Woodbridge Inn* (car park available for use), walk down the drive to the start of the Coalport Bridge

Behind you, tucked back, but clearly visible, is the former Great Western Railway Station of the Severn Valley Railway, opened in 1862, one of two railway stations that Coalport once boasted. The building is a private dwelling now. In the garden is a restored GWR coach, used as a holiday let.

LEFT: *Woodbridge Inn in the 1930s*
RIGHT: *GWR Coalport Station*

2 Walk over the Coalport Bridge with its former toll house on the right.

The name of The Woodbridge pub tells us a little bit about Coalport Bridge. It was formerly called the Preens Eddy Bridge and was originally built of wood with stone abutments

You can learn more about Coalport Bridge in walk no 3 on Page 46
See story: *'Miss Green, the Tollkeeper's Daughter'* Page 47

3 Just on the other side of the bridge, look out for a wooden gate and sign indicating 'The Silkin Way' on the left (this is a local long-distance walk and cycle route which starts here and traverses Telford to the north at Wellington). Pass through the gate, down a gently sloping path. After about 100 metres there is a T-junction. Turn right to pass under the railway bridge ahead, reconstructed in 1995.

4 Continue on this path which passes the site (no remains) of the former station of the London & North Western Railway (LNWR) branch line, on the left just before the road bridge ahead.

Coalport East Station (LNWR)

The LNWR built their branch line from Wellington to Coalport and it opened for passengers in June 1861. For about a hundred years it played a vital role in the life of the community here, until its closure in 1952 (ten years later for freight).

MEMORIES OF A COALPORT RAILWAYMAN'S SON

Things That Went On

During the Second World War the ammunition trains at Coalport East Station had their own dedicated siding. I can remember the first black men I ever saw in my life were American GIs guarding those ammunition trains. In those early days, as well, there used to be a cattle dock where the local farmers brought their livestock ready to be transported to market. The cowherd that brought them down the lane can't have been very good because I can remember on more than one occasion cattle pushing their way through the garden hedge and deciding to have a meal off the front lawn!

On other occasions, bearing in mind as a family we all got free travel, we were sometimes allowed to ride the footplate on the journey to Madeley where we went to school. Ride the footplate! Can you imagine that now? My brother I recall used to throw such a tantrum if he wasn't allowed onto the footplate. Sometimes we rode the footplate together, and he was even allowed to operate the vacuum brakes up at Madeley, all under the guidance, of course, of the driver! They did quite a few things in those days that they'd never be able to do now. But they weren't just irregular things, but considerate things as well. For example, in the severe winter of 1946/1947 when there were really heavy snowfalls, the afternoon train crew realised that the morning crew would never get out of the

station at Coalport, unless they did something. So, they volunteered to run the train up and down to Madeley all night long to keep the line clear!

Story of the Newspaper Boy Dog

The antics involving our pet dog, a Jack Russell, always used to amuse me as a child. If my father was at work, the dog would simply carry on sleeping on the mat in the living room, because he knew the evening newspaper would come home with my father. But if my father was off-duty and in his armchair (perhaps asleep!) at about five o'clock the dog would suddenly spring up and make for the door. It was usually ajar, but if it wasn't, he'd whine the house down until somebody opened it. And then he'd go charging off down the steps and across the garden. Two minutes later he'd be back with the paper in his mouth, picked up from the embankment where the guard - by prior arrangement - would have carefully thrown it from the passing train! Talk about a personal paper delivery without even getting out of your armchair!

The End

They closed the LNWR in 1952 to passengers - I walked to Madeley to get the last train back and I still have the ticket as a memento - but freight carried on for another 10 years. The Severn Valley Line of the Great Western Railway (GWR) on the opposite bank of the river closed the following year in 1963. I have memories of some very sad scenes of dereliction of the old LNWR station in the 1960s with the track rusted and overgrown and with its abandoned trucks.

Pass under the bridge. On the other side the path fronts some railway cottages on the right hand side, before coming to a short flight of steps on the left.

5 Go up the steps which lead to a tarmacked drive. Directly ahead of you, you will see another set of steps leading into this western section of Sutton Wood.

The woodland here is predominantly larch but with some mixed deciduous species. The larch has been thinned to allow the new steps and path and the intention is eventually to return the woodland to an entirely mixed deciduous form with native species, in order to increase habitat and species diversity. There are, indeed, already new plantings of oak and hazel, a traditional coppice tree.

COPPICING

Coppicing is a traditional 'cut and come' again technique which provides a sustainable way of managing woodland. The process involves cutting the understorey every seven to ten years (a longer cycle for some species) to harvest a crop of small diameter poles used in a variety of craft products such as hurdles and fences, chairs, gates, hedge stakes, tools, baskets

and trugs. The list is extensive. Coppicing is one of the most wildlife-friendly forms of woodland management, and hazel coppice provides a rare habitat for several species such as dormouse, blackcap and several species of butterfly.

Dormouse, extremely shy species identified closely with hazel coppice

Keep on the path, taking the steps option to the right. Soon you will come to a set of steps to the left and a boardwalk straight on. You can take either direction. Straight on, you will see two small footbridges, to the left only one. Nearby there is a magnificent veteran oak tree. Continue on up a sereies of steps eventually reaching a gate. Pass through and cross the tarmacked lane to another gate immediately opposite, with a further flight of steps continuing up. Take these.

6 You will finally come to another gate, exiting onto a wide unmade track. Turn right here and follow the track. Eventually you will come to a T-junction.

7 More or less directly opposite is a stile leading into the heart of the woodland. You should take this, but before doing so, notice - just to the right of the stile - a small rectangular pool behind a screen of willow and scrub vegetation.

Whilst Sutton Wood is crossed by a series of springs, the woodland edge pool is a rarity here and provides an invaluable wetland habitat. It is home to a variety of amphibious and other aquatic life, including all three native British species of newt - smooth, palmate and great-crested.

Improvement works to create new steps and paths in Sutton Wood 2004

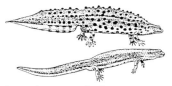

Smooth newt, male above

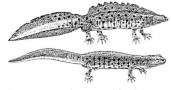

Palmate newt, male above

Pass over the stile and continue on the main path. After about 30-40 metres there is a path off to the left, subsequently over farmland, leading to the old community of Sutton Maddock. Our broad path continues on.

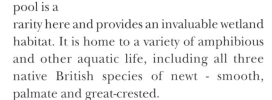

Great creasted newt, male above

Sutton Wood is classified as 'ancient replanted woodland'. There is plenty of historical evidence to suggest that Wenlock Priory had holdings in the area during early medieval times, with adjacent and nearby field names suggesting more extensive forest cover from earlier times. On the ground, there are several 'indicator' species of ancient semi-natural woodland, such as dogs mercury, wood anemones and bluebells. Over a long period of time the woodland here has been put to commercial use with a series of large-scale fellings, the last being that of dead elm during the 1970s by Telford Development Corporation. This was followed by replanting with a mixture of conifers and broadleaves (eg sweet chestnut) among preserved older examples of limes, ash and occasional oak, cherry and holly.

Bluebells

Continue along the path until you are required to take a fairly sharp right turn.

8 The walk opens out here and the path quickly comes to a junction. Turn left when you will reach a T-junction. Take the left fork, slightly uphill which widens to a pleasant leafy track. **[Consult walk map]**

After about a100 metres, you will notice a fine view of the square tower of Sutton Maddock church across fields off to the left. After another 100 metres the path dips gently, offering clear views in autumn and winter of the large Severn Trent water treatment plant on the south side of the river, visible in the distance on the right.

> The treatment plant is on the site of an old brickworks and tilery at Gitchfield. In 1940 a local Coalport man, George Gough, was involved in an extraordinary act of 'ordinary heroism', the sort of act which in wartime was not uncommon, but remarkable when one pauses for a moment to reflect on what was involved. In this case what he did was acknowledged at the highest level.

You can read 'The Gitchfield Incident - News from 1940' on Page 62

The path eventually comes to a point where it peters out but with a steep flight of steps down on the right.

9 Go down the steps which will bring you to a lower path.

10 Turn right here and continue on this lovely woodland loop until you reach a point corresponding to Step 8 [Consult walk map]

Female blackcap showing its distinctive red cap

11 Here you need to turn left, and left again, down a gently sloping grassy woodland ride. There is the delightful sound of running water hereabouts from the springs that cross this section of wood. You may also find several large inspection covers to the Severn Trent pipework which also crosses the area. Carry on down and you will come to a gate and stile.

12 Pass over the stile onto a concrete track and turn right. Approximately 80 metres on, you will come to another stile on the left.

13 Pass over the stile into another section of Sutton Wood, characterised initially by beech and field maple. The path comes to a fork after about 150 metres. Take the right hand fork, a broad grassy ride which soon comes to a stile onto a broad track.

14 You may recognise this track as that you came down to start this part of the walk. Turn left. After about 200-300 metres you will come to the gate on the left which you used earlier.

15 Pass through the gate back into woodland and then down the series of constructed steps you came up, leading eventually back to the Coalport Bridge and your starting point at the *Woodbridge Inn*.

'THE GITCHFIELD INCIDENT - NEWS FROM 1940'

One night in October 1940, a cluster of wayward incendiary bombs fell in the Coalport area during a raid by the Luftwaffe on Ironbridge Power Station. One of those bombs landed on the roof of a building in the tile factory at Gitchfield - which is now the site of the Severn Trent water treatment works.

An item in the local paper soon afterwards reported that 34-year old George Gough had rendered the bomb harmless "at some risk to himself". That was something of an under-statement in that the type of German incendiary in this case was designed to ignite on impact, scattering fizzing, white-hot lumps of thermite filling - laced with wax or latex to help them stick to anything in their path. If that wasn't enough to make the eyes water, a nose-cone filled with a charge of TNT could be added to the bomb and set to detonate at a random timing after impact - to discourage fire-fighters from tackling the incendiary before it could do damage.

As an Air Raid Patrol (ARP) warden, George would have been well aware of what he was taking on, so it's reasonable to wonder just what motivated him to risk his life in that way, to save, perhaps, a few stacks of tiles from being scorched. Readers of that newspaper account might have asked the same question at the time, although - due to the need for secrecy in wartime - they would have been none the wiser. But what George knew from his 'day job', driving a shunting-engine around the Works' railway sidings, was that the building under threat that night did not hold tiles. It was packed with ammunition and explosives.

CONTINUED OVERLEAF

It was common practice during the Second World War for stocks of munitions to be dispersed around the country in unassuming locations close to rural railway routes. Gitchfield, on the Great Western Railway's Severn Valley Line, was one of those sites. George Gough would have been keenly aware that his wife and young family were asleep close by - at their home in Gitchfield Cottages. He would also have seen the risk to everyone else in the area, which was more densely populated than it is today.

So, it was not only George's raw bravery, but also the prevention of a potentially catastrophic disaster which was recognized when he was presented with a vellum scroll embossed with the Royal Arms and carrying the following text in copperplate manuscript:

By the KING'S Order the name of
George Gough,
Locomotive Driver, Coalport, Shropshire
was published in the London Gazette on
17th January 1941
as commended for brave conduct in Civil Defence.
I am charged to record His Majesty's high appreciation of the service rendered.

Prime Minister and First Lord
of the Treasury

"By the KING's Order the name George Gough, Locomotive Driver, Coalport, Shropshire, was published in the London Gazette on 17 January 1941 as commended for brave conduct in Civil Defence. I am charged to record His Majesty's high appreciation of the service rendered."

The document is signed: "Winston S Churchill", in the 'Great Man's' own hand, above the legend: "Prime Minister and First Lord of the Treasury"

George Gough's son - also named George - still lives in Coalport. He and his sister, Joyce Garbett, are justifiably proud of their father and the framed commendation is a treasured memento of his exploit. We too should thank George Senior. Without his bravery, bits of Coalport might still be being scraped from the surrounding countryside - and, George Junior being a local farmer, we wouldn't be enjoying his wonderful eggs and other produce!

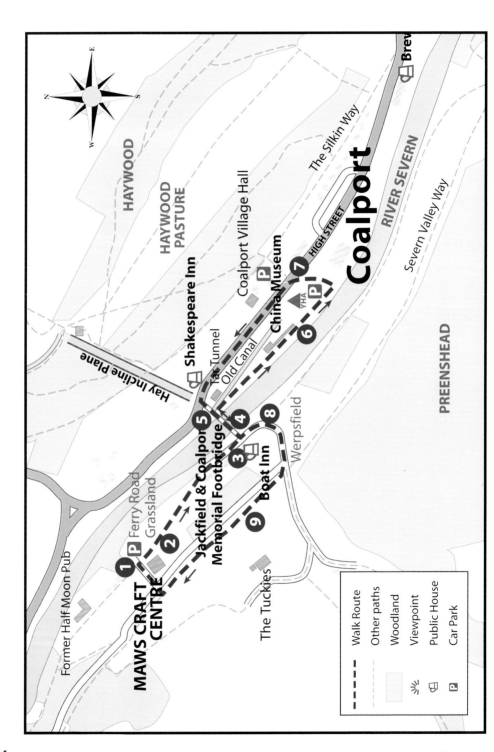

Coalport

HAYWOOD

HAYWOOD PASTURE

The Silkin Way

RIVER SEVERN

Brew

Severn Valley Way

PREENSHEAD

Coalport Village Hall

China Museum

HIGH STREET

Shakespeare Inn

Tar Tunnel

Old Canal

Hay Incline Plane

Jackfield & Coalport Memorial Footbridge

Boat Inn

Werpsfield

Ferry Road

Grassland

MAWS CRAFT CENTRE

Former Half Moon Pub

The Tuckies

1 2 3 4 5 6 7 8 9

YHA

—— Walk Route

— — Other paths

Woodland

Viewpoint

Public House

Car Park

Walk No 5

Maw's Craft Centre to The Boat Inn to the Memorial Bridge to Coalport China Museum to The Werps

This short 'clean-shoe' walk offers an insight into some of the 18C/19C history of both Jackfield and Coalport. Starting at **Maw's Craft Centre** (car park nearby), home of the former Tile Works, the path moves on to **The Boat Inn** and thence over the **Jackfield & Coalport Memorial footbridge** offering views of the remarkable **Hay Inclined Plane**. The walk travels along a section of the **old Coalport canal** to the China Museum and Youth Hostel, both housed in former buildings of the **China Works**, before concluding by passing back over the footbridge, through part of the **Werps district** of Jackfield back to the Craft Centre.

Accessibility: Shoes are perfectly adequate for this short walk, which apart from the steps on either side of the Memorial Bridge, is largely on the level. There are no stiles but there are river and canal stretches – children will need to be supervised.

Key Features: Industrial and social history, archaeology.

Length & Time: 1½ km – about ¾ hour

Public Transport: Buses to Jackfield and Coalport.

Refreshments: Maw's Craft Centre café, the Boat Inn, The Shakespeare Inn

Toilets: Maw's Craft Centre, Youth Hostel, China Museum.

1 Maw's Craft Centre is the starting point for this walk and is well worth a visit, either now or at the end of the walk. The Centre utilises a number of the surviving buildings of the former Maw & Co., tile manufacturers.

Maw & Co. were once the largest decorative tile manufacturers in the world, with a workforce of several hundred, and producing millions tiles a year. Something of the sheer size and complexity of the factory can be gauged from the inset aerial photo of Jackfield taken in the summer of 1948.

More fascinating information about Maw's can be obtained from walk No 1 on Page 21

2 With the car park on your left, continue on the footpath which runs down the left hand side of the Maw's building. There is a pleasant area of amenity grassland on your left.

Much of the green area consists of huge quantities of ceramic tile waste dumped from the former tile works. Indeed, ahead of you on the right hand side, issuing from the old factory wall, you can see a wooden chute down which the tile waste was poured in to a waiting horse-drawn cart.

The aerial photograph of 1948 also shows there were cottages on the land, and the Maw's canteen, known as the 'Mess Room' which once served as the Village Hall, and also a temporary home for the Jackfield Brass Band. There was even a tennis court. Such examples indicate something of the commitment of the company to the social welfare of its employees and the wider community.

See story: *'Jackfield Brass Band'* Page 52

The footpath soon becomes Ferry Road.

3 Ferry Road opens out in front of *The Boat Inn* on the right and the Jackfield & Coalport Memorial Bridge on the left.

The Boat Inn is one of only three surviving pubs in Jackfield of the many which used to characterise this riverside community. It was officially licensed in 1840 but, as was common in the Gorge, was probably operating as an illegal brewhouse and brothel long before that.

You can learn more about this interesting public house in walk no 1 Page 23

4 Now pass over the recently renovated Jackfield & Coalport Memorial Bridge.

Jackfield Ferry

The footbridge, a vital link between the north and south sides of the river, has a remarkable story behind it. A ferry had operated at this fast-flowing point on the river since the 1790s, principally to ferry workers from Jackfield and those from Broseley to the China Works at Coalport. The boat usually carried a maximum of 40 people and operated by means of a chain or wire rope attached to the top of the mast and secured by an anchor in the centre of the river upstream. In 1799 the ferry sank, drowning 28 people, all from the China Works. Even from the early 20C it was a matter of public discussion to replace this means of getting across the river with a footbridge, which eventually came about in 1922. The story of the bridge can be read on page 68, told by a contemporary of the time.

5 On the other side of the footbridge, you come to a pleasant Canal Basin, a restored section of the Coalport canal built by William Reynolds in the late 18C. Looking straight ahead, you will also see the road bridge and how a remarkable construction called the Hay Inclined Plane passes under the bridge.

For more than a hundred years the Hay Inclined Plane moved goods and raw materials in a matter of minutes up and down between the East Shropshire canal up at Blist's Hill and the River Severn, a difference in levels equivalent to 27 conventional locks.

You can visit the remains of the Engine House and chimney of the Hay Inclined Plane and learn more about the construction in walk no 2 on Page 37

Just to the right of the Hay Inclined Plane on the road front is *The Shakespeare Inn*, many of whose customers during the 19C were workers from Blists Hill at the top of the incline and also china workers until the factory closed down in 1926.

A Most Useful, Unusual War Memorial

Opening of the bridge in 1922

"Not long after the War [First World War] had ended, there was a great movement in the area to construct a memorial to all those who'd been killed. The people in Broseley decided on an obelisk; those in Ironbridge opted for a bronze statue of a soldier. But in Jackfield we wanted something more lasting. The idea came up that we needed to replace the ferry crossing, so it was suggested that we build a bridge there as a useful memorial to the fallen of both Jackfield and Coalport. A fund-raising committee was formed whose members had all lost sons in the War. Jack Harrison, the baker, was on the committee, as was George 'Plum' Hadley, the driver of the LNWR Coalport 'Dodger'. He was one of the key instigators of the bridge.

Funds were raised by band concerts and fetes, and also by collections. Everyone gave freely, even the tileworks owners helped out where they could. There was always a strong community spirit in the village in those days.

By 1921, the builders had put a framework over the river with a single width length of planks resting on top. The foreman in charge of the construction was Mr. Swain who wore a trilby hat.

As kids we'd wait till the evening, when the workmen had gone, and then cross the river on the planks. One dark night I crossed the bridge over to Coalport with my friends, but came back on my own. As I walked over the bridge the wind picked up and and a gust nearly blew me into the river! I was so scared that I crawled the rest of the way on my hands and knees.

When I reached the Jackfield side all I could see in front of me were a man's legs. I looked up to see Mr Swain glaring down at me and he wasn't very pleased!"

The bridge was completed and came into use in 1922. After the Second World War it was rededicated to the fallen of both World Wars.

It was completely renovated in 2000.

Also on the other side of the canal, to the right of the Incline, you will see signs to another intriguing construction, The Tar Tunnel.

In 1786, as part of his plans for developing the area, the remarkable ironmaster and entrepreneur, William Reynolds, tried to drive a canal directly from the riverbank to the coal mines at Blist's Hill, further to the north. After about 275 metres he struck a spring of natural bitumen. Reynolds abandoned his tunnelling at this point in time, recognising the commercial value of the discovery. Outside the tunnel entrance he erected cauldrons to process the bitumen into a variety of products, such as pitch for timber preservation, fuel oil, and medicinal preparations for rheumatic and skin complaints. Initially, the tunnel yielded hundreds of gallons of tar a day, but by 1820 there was no more than a trickle, which ceased altogether in 1843.

Walk on the path to the right of the canal which eventually brings you close to the buildings of the former China Works and one of the elegant bottle kilns used in pottery manufacture.

6 A small footbridge crosses the canal which you should take. Turn right and walk through to the car park with the main museum on the right and the John Rose Building, now a Youth Hostel, on the left.

ABOVE: *Coalport China Works and canal*

BELOW: *Engraving of the old China Woks*

Throughout the 19C the name of John Rose was firmly linked with china manufacture at Coalport. He was an extremely talented potter and the first to establish a china works on this site at a time when William Reynolds was developing the area in the late 18C. The banks of Reynolds' canal provided an ideal location for this type of manufactory, since coal could easily be transported from the coalfields via the canal, used to fire the kilns, whilst the proximity of the river Severn - later the railway system - provided the means of shipping the finished products to their markets, at home and abroad. The China Works continued for more than a hundred years, closing eventually on this site in 1926, although Coalport china is still made in the Potteries. Today, most of the surviving buildings of the China Works, including the distinctive bottle kilns, form part of the Coalport China Museum.

John Rose Building

7 Exit from the car park, past the Youth Hostel on your left, into Coalport High Street. As you walk on for a few metres, notice just how many cast iron windows there are in the John Rose Building, designed to let in the maximum amount of light for the often delicate and meticulous work involved in decorating the china. After a few metres you will come to the end of the building and a turning off to the left. The path ahead leads back to the canal over the little footbridge. Take this and retrace your steps back to the Jackfield & Coalport Memorial Bridge. Pass over this, back to the *Boat Inn* on the south side of the river.

8 At *The Boat Inn* turn left, past the beer garden, following the road round to the right.

> The area you are now in is known as the Werps which in the 19C and first half of the 20C was a thriving district of Jackfield in its own right. There were many houses and gardens, arranged in the form of a "Square", and two pubs, one of which was 'The Duke of Wellington'. As you walk up the road, you will see two modern dwellings on the left hand side, the site of the former pub with its bowling green. Apart from a few surviving dwellings, virtually the whole of the Werps was demolished in the 1950s as part of 'slum clearance' and with it another historic part of Jackfield was lost.

Continue on up the road, turning right before the railway bridge.

> The road you have been walking on is known as The Tuckies Road, leading to another of the many districts of Jackfield, and yet another which has suffered greatly through loss of its buildings to the point where it is no longer a community in its own right. The road itself is interesting – certainly important enough to have warranted the building of a bridge to take the Severn Valley Railway above – in that it was the main route for workers from Broseley (further south) and The Tuckies making their way down to the ferry to work at the China Works in Coalport.

9 Continue on the road ahead of you, being careful of the occasional car which will pass this way. The road is now running parallel to the former railway line on your left. Indeed the road you are on also served as the railway sidings for the Maw's Tile Manufactory a little further up on the right.

> The Severn Valley Way, now a major recreational route for walkers and cyclists, was established along the bed of the old Severn Valley

Railway (SVR). This served Jackfield and Coalport for a hundred years, before closure in the early 1960s.

A few more metres on, if you look left you will see a handsome house (now three dwellings) known as 'The Tuckies'.

The Tuckies is the oldest house of any size within the Gorge, and was at one time the home of the influential ironmaster and founder of Coalport, William Reynolds.

Walk No 1 is a delightful walk which passes close to The Tuckies and where you can learn more about this interesting building (see Page 28).

In an adjacent field you may also catch sight of a curious circular structure which was actually a reservoir built by Maw & Co to supply water for mixing with the clay to make 'slip' for its tiles.

Follow the road you are on back to the entrance of Maw's Craft Centre and your starting point.

Acknowledgements

Thanks are due to the following organisations and individuals for permission to use photographs, images and text in the booklet:

Andy Purcell: Green woodpecker *Page 38*
Shropshire Archives: early-18C map of 'Jack-Field' *Page 3*
Pauline Hannigan: The Severn Trow *Page 16*, Severn Trow Advert *Page18*, Three in A Coracle *Page 54*, The General Gordon Inn *Page 18*, Henry Potts *Page 25*
Cambridge University Photographic Library: Aerial Photograph of Jackfield *Page 23 & 66*
Ironbridge Gorge Museum Trust: Jackfield/Coalport ferry circa 1900-1910 *Page 50 & 67*, Flooded Boat Inn 1925 *Page 24*, Coalport by H. Clements *Page 26*, Portrait John Rose *Page 9 & 35*, Hay Inclined Plane late 19C *Page 37*, GWR Coalport Station *Page 10 & 57*, Opening Jackfield & Coalport Memorial Bridge 1922 *Page 11 & 68*, Portrait William Reynolds *Page 8*, Close of Coalport China Works 1926 *Page 10*, Late 19C Engraving of Coalport China Works *Page 7 & 69*, Jackfield Ware Mug, Jackfield Tile Museum, *Page 4*, Early Brickworks *Page 4 & back cover*, Coalport China plates *Page 9*, Coalport China teapot *Page 49*, Maws tiles *Page 22*
Graham Banks: 'Coalport Dodger' in Coalport East Station *Page 10* circa 1950, Bert (Bob) Banks with sons *Page 41*, 'Memories of a Coalport Railwayman's Son' *Pages 41 & 58* and 'Miss Green: The Tollkeeper's Daughter' *page 47* based upon reminiscences by Graham Banks
Moyra & Tony Dolman: Portrait Frank Poole *Page 53*, Luke Dolman with Eustace Rogers *Page 53*, 'The Gitchfield Incident' *Page 62*,
Paul France: Jackfield Brass Band 1926 *Page 52*
Michael Pooley: Retaining wall of old saggars, *Page 5*, St Mary's Church, Jackfield *Page 16*, Boat Inn *Page 51*, Tuckies House with Maw's water reservoir *Page 28*, Tony Mugridge with former Jackfield 'Halt' as shed *Page 31*, Hand-made bricks *Page 31*, Jackfield's 'wooden road' *Page 32*, The Brewery Inn *Page 39*, Maw's encaustic tile *Page 44*, Maw's decorative tile *Page 6*, Entrance to former Maw's Tile Works *Page 44*, John Rose Building *Page 69*, Restored section of

Coalport canal *Page 69*, Shakespeare Inn *Page 48*, Line drawing Bridge Inn, Coalport Page, Woodbridge Inn *Page 46*, walker in woodland *Page 61*, Memorial Bridge *Page 68*, Jackfield Village Hall *Page 15*, the Half Moon Jug *Page 21*, The Severn Trow *Page 16*
Neville John Anderson: Portrait General Gordon of Khartoum *Page 25*
Mike Ashton: Family walking by Maws *front cover*, Maws Craft Centre *front cover & Page 44*, Coalport Bridge *Page 26 & front cover*, Hazel Catkins *Page 27*, football *Page 30*, Coalport Tollhouse *Page 47*, Maws Waste Chute *Page 51*, Native British newts *Page 60*, Memorial Bridge *Page 68*
Tony Mugridge: Reminiscences of Norman Hudson *Pages 53 & 68* repr. in 'Coracles, Coracles!' pub AJ Mugridge 1997, Reminiscence of Harry Hudson ibid *Page 52*, Reminiscences of Jack Bill and Jack Griffiths ibid *Page 30*, 'The Mekest' *Page 20*, information from 'The Village of Jackfield' pub. AJ Mugridge 1997, 'The Half Moon Jug' *Page 21* repr. ibid
Mary Oliver: 'Memories of Growing Up In Jackfield' *Page 14* based upon reminiscences of M. Oliver
Jean Edwards: 'Animal Bones' *Page 36* based upon reminiscence of J. Edwards
Chris Wenlock: Sutton Wood Works *Page 60*, Common spotted orchid *Page 45*, bluebells *Page 60*, coppicing and coppice stool *Page 59*
Glen Bishton: Blackcap *Front Cover & Page 61*
Pete Boardman: Ringlet butterfly *Page 36*,
Shropshire Wildlife Trust: Dormouse Page 59
BBC: Harry Rogers Demonstrating Use of Coracle *Page 53*
WA Camwell: Coalport East Station with locomotive *Page 57*
Larry Jones: Coppiced stool and Larry Jones coppicing *Page 59*
George Gough & Joyce Garbett: Wedding photo of George Gough (senior) *Page 62*, 'King's Order' Certificate *Page 63*